BEST

OF

TIMOTHY GAGER

POEMS, ESSAYS, AND STORIES 2002—2022

ISBN: 978-1-945917-78-3

Printed in the United States of America
Cover Design: Sheila Smallwood

Also by Timothy Gager:

The Same Corner of the Bar (Ibbetson Street Press, 2003)
We Needed a Night Out (Cyberwit Publications, 2005)
This is Where You Go When You are Gone (Cervena Barva Press, 2008)
These poems are not pink fluffy clouds (Propaganda Press, 2008)
Anti-Social Network (Red Neck Press, 2013)
The Shutting Door (Ibbetson Street Press, 2013)
Chief Jay Strongbow is Real (Big Table, 2017)
Every Day There is Something About Elephants (Big Table, 2018)
Spreading Like Wildflowers (Big Table, 2019)
2020 Poems (Big Table, 2021)
Joe the Salamander (Golden Antelope Press, 2022)

BIG TABLE Publishing

"Making other books jealous since 2004"

Big Table Publishing Company
Boston, MA & San Francisco, CA
www.bigtablepublishing.com

In gratitude...
to those who believed enough in me
to fill up this anthology:

Robin Stratton, Big Table Publishing Company
Betsy Delmonico, Golden Antelope Publishing
Doug Holder, Ibbetson Street Press
Rusty Barnes, Red Neck Press
Leah Angstrom, Propaganda Press
Gloria Mindock, Cervena Barva Press

For my family, friends, and those waiting
for a miracle to happen. There is a solution. May you
find it, or at least some kindness
along the way.

Table of Contents

Foreword by Robin Stratton
Introduction by Timothy Gager

GROUNDED, New poems, 2022

SECRETS AND COMPARTMENTS,
New flash fictions, 2019-2023

from THE SAME CORNER OF THE BAR

from WE NEEDED A NIGHT OUT

from THIS IS WHERE YOU GO
WHEN YOU ARE GONE

from THESE POEMS ARE NOT PINK CLOUDS

from TREATING A SICK ANIMAL

ESSAY

from ANTI-SOCIAL NETWORK

ESSAY

from THE SHUTTING DOOR

from CHIEF JAY STRONGBOW IS REAL

NOVEL EXCERPT *from The Thursday Appointments of Bill Sloan*

NOVEL EXCERPT *from Grand Slams: A Coming of Eggs Story*

from EVERYDAY THERE IS SOMETHING ABOUT ELEPHANTS

from SPREADING LIKE WILDFLOWERS

from 2020 POEMS

ESSAY

NOVEL EXCERPT *from Joe the Salamander*

FOREWORD

by Robin Stratton

Tim Gager is a lot of things: poet, novelist, magazine editor, director of the popular Dire Reading Series, and beloved mascot in the Boston literary scene where he contributes his energy to supporting and cheering on all his writing friends. He's talented, funny, charming, adorable, helpful, and a dozen years sober. During Covid, while the rest of us stayed home and watched re-runs of *Gray's Anatomy* and *Downton Abbey* and maybe dashed off a poem or two, he wrote an entire volume, Amazon's #1 best-selling *2020 Poems*. With the literary world basically shut down, he reinvented his reading series by becoming a Zoom host, and then uploaded all of the readings on YouTube. Of course he was also hard at work on his latest novel, *Joe the Salamander*, a sweetly-sad, funny and heartfelt story about a boy with autism.

It was during this time that I contacted him and asked if he'd be willing to let us publish a Best-of collection. Please understand how unusual it is for Big Table Publishing Company to solicit manuscripts. We get a lot of them, why do we go looking for more?

Because it's Tim Gager. It's *Tim Gager*.

When I started Big Table Publishing Company in 2004, it was a modest endeavor, primarily aimed at helping my writing friends get published. I under-estimated the excitement of a new indie press in the community, and was surprised that we were buried in submissions almost from the start. And as I became immersed in the scene, I kept hearing the name Tim Gager. *Have you met Tim Gager yet? You haven't'? Oh, you have to meet him!*

In September 2012, I attended the "100,000 Poets" event hosted by Dedham's Poet Laureate, Christopher Reilley. As a fledging writer of poetry (I dared not refer to myself as a "poet;" I still don't) I was happy to see some of my writing friends, including two local favorites known as "the two Jenns"—Jennifer Jean and Jennifer Martelli. Chris tapped my arm and said, "There's Tim Gager," and I looked and sure enough, there he was: tall and lanky, smiling warmly. I said, "Oh!" He said, "Hi," and held out his hand and we shook. And that is how I finally met Tim Gager.

We became friends. I was over the top excited when he asked if Big Table would consider his first novel, *The Thursday Appointments of Bill Sloan.* It's about a fame-lusting psychologist who wants to have his own show, like Dr. Phil, and the disastrous consequences when he gets it. *Thursday Appointments* was Big Table's hottest seller in 2014.

Tim went back to poetry and short fiction for his next two books, both published by Big Table: *Chief Jay Strongbow is Real* (2017) and *Every Day There is Something about Elephants* (2018.) When we threw a book launch for *Elephants,* I did something I'd never done before or since: I asked him if I could read one of his stories. Such nerve! What if he was planning to read it? It didn't matter, I couldn't help it, I *had* to be the one to present that story to the crowd. "Jack" is a brilliant, tragic, sparsely, masterfully written story about a cop whose wife is murdered, and I love the last paragraph so much that it almost makes me cry:

> Jack has nightmares of yellow tape he can't cross. Jack spends a lot of time on the sofa. It works like a handcuff. Friends bring dinner. There is food on the table. Jack takes off his hat. "Never marry a cop," Jack used to kid. Jack washes his creased face. He says, "Oh God, Oh my God."

Tim's next novel was *Grand Slams, a Coming of Eggs Story*. Loosely based on his own teen years, it's about an ill-adjusted, going-nowhere kid who winds up working at a diner. I loved the review on Amazon that called it "funny, tense, and tender."

Spreading Like Wildflowers was released just before the pandemic hit, the title sounding like the last breath of fresh air before the world stopped breathing, and in "The Miracles of Recovery," Tim asks himself with a trace of wonder,

> Who would have thought salvation is no longer found in the piss jars in old isolated bedrooms?

Then it was 2020. Tim, proudly sober at that point for ten years, was alone with his roommates (two rabbits: Alice and Bertie), and was deeply grieving the loss of his mother who had died just a few months earlier, and the decline of his father, who had moved to Maryland and because of COVID, was un-visitable—a gloomy set of circumstances that made most of us reach for a second glass of wine at night. But the true poet embraces emotions, whether joyful or the shittiest time of one's entire life, and that's what Tim did:

> If you're weak of mind
> this poem is not a holiday;
> it does not twinkle, nor
>
> are its words lights from a city,
> observed upon the descent—
> each, a pushpin of hope.

Completing and securing a publishing contract for *Joe the Salamander* and then busting his ass promoting it didn't seem to slow Tim down at all, and when he submitted his *Best of* manuscript, I was amazed at how much new material was there. As always, I felt that tug of envy, and I am not ashamed to admit it. I especially love the way his chaotic thoughts make a solid landing in such a powerfully calm, insightful place in "God and You:"

> Take a trip if you want to come up
> to celebrate 6 AM.
> It's been 20 years since
> we stayed in Yellowstone,
> and, yeah, I'm still struggling:
> maybe nine months-six months-three months.
>
> One month is when you're coming?
> I love you even with *that* mouth.
> Can you hear me at this distance

saying, *I don't need people*
I can stay in my room.
But I don't have to be that person anymore.

If the title "Christmas 2019" makes you think you
are going to be reading about fluffy snowflakes and
kissing 'neath the mistletoe...nope! He has something
else in mind, this master of grabbing your heart;
instead of twisting it, he releases it and launches it into
a beautiful, sacred place:

Stunned awake by ring tone
—nothing good comes of—that

nurse asking if you'd like
to say a final goodbye

as your mother lies dying in a hospice bed.
Maybe they're only keeping her alive

so you can drive to Harbor House at
midnight, because hospice is respectful

the same way a neighbor will
later send you a sympathy card.

So, you tell the nurse, No
because you have said

goodbye every day
for the past two months,

sat there at the bedside, heard
her whisper she wasn't scared

of what comes after. She said,
you know, one time,

she smelled the scent
of roses in the dead of Winter.

Working with Tim Gager has surely been a highlight of my career as editor of Big Table Publishing Company. Being his friend, a highlight of my life. When you read this book, you'll understand. Because it's Tim Gager. It's *Tim Gager*.

Robin Stratton, January 2023
San Francisco, CA

Introduction
by Timothy Gager

I'm often quite strong willed to work with. I have ideas and visions regarding my work, and I have a difficult time letting go.

Soon after Big Table Publishing Company released an anthology of Doug Holder's greatest works, *The Essential Doug Holder*, I was asked by Big Table, my publisher of many years, if I would be interested in releasing *The Essential Timothy Gager*, a compilation of what they considered my best. To be so honored, wouldn't you think I would just go with whatever they want?

Well, it is words and the meaning of words which are important, so this is where my head went when I heard the word "essential," which is defined by the Oxford Dictionary as: *absolutely necessary, extremely important.*

I don't feel essential. I never have. Food, water, oxygen, and human contact. Essential. Essential. Essential. Essential. My poems, my fiction, my excerpts. Non-essential. Non-essential. Non-essential. Important to me? Yes. Important to others? I've discovered there are a few people I've made some sort of mark on, but I've never been essential. I am even classified in my job as a non-essential employee, but I am essential enough to draw a paycheck for the past twenty-plus years. My sperm may fit that description as it was essential in producing my children. That fits the definition pretty well, but, also not as a title.

I've done an honest assessment of the work included in this anthology, and while all are the "best" of any given period of my writing or particular publication, I don't feel they are *essential*.

At one point I felt different about my place in the world. I, as a human being, was very, very, essential, but only in my own mind. Damn, how essential I thought I was! Whatever I wanted, I felt I deserved in one way or another. If things didn't happen there had to be someone at fault or some dislike of me.

I also had the important task of figuring out every motivation of every person in the universe and create a narrative around it; my own jaded narrative which was 100% correct, of course. Everything had to be exactly what I thought, because I held this essential central place and *my* world revolved around it. If it was a square peg in a round hole, I would keep trying until I could jam it in. Everything in that world was black and white, and I held the dye. This is what happens when you appoint yourself while being self-important and dripping with ego. I had a lot to learn.

I got sober in 2010, but it was only when I learned some humility, did sober life kick in as something enjoyable. I welcome you reader, to play a game. Remember those puzzles in children's magazines where you would find the differences in two illustrations or photographs and circle them in pencil? It is a game you can play when you read this. I challenge you to find the differences in the work written before 2010, versus the ones written after. Some of the work appearing in books published after 2010 have poems or stories written before 2010, so it can get tricky. Replay review might be necessary.

I am thrilled that new, unseen work is included. When I asked Big Table Publishing's editor Robin Stratton if there was room for any new poems and stories, she was enthusiastic. Little did she know that I had nearly an entire book, over 150 pages of new pieces! What's more, I wanted them to be in the beginning. She asked if she could present the material chronologically, at the end. I said I'd prefer to start with them, and she said, "Okay, that's fine." Many years into my life as a writer, I can tell you that it is support and encouragement, including this invitation from Robin, that has kept me going, and keeps me willing to write more—and not quit.

I am extremely grateful to Big Table Publishing Company for honoring me by publishing this volume. It humbles me greatly, to have something like this in my hands. I hope you can feel that energy as it sits in your hands right now, and although it is not "essential," I hope it will somehow leave an impression.

"Live 24-7," Timothy Gager

GROUNDED

"It is the way you move from side to side
like a waltz slowed in time."
~ New poems, 2021-2022

Runway

I wrote these words as the aircraft lifted.
What I would have said if you were here.
I cannot call to tell you—you won't pick up
or send a tepid-feeling not-answered text, but

I can send this poem,
these words I cannot speak,
aloud as building engines roar.

Remember the last time
that we both took flight?

Purple Robe

dark curls billowed
onto the shoulders of
the cozy, plush robe
which opened majestically
like a theater's curtain.
First Act of Opening Night.

Although I Never Called You Beautiful

I remember the way a ringlet rests
Naturally coiled around your ear

or when your lips burst from flat to smile,
softly twisting breaths alive within mine.

It is the way you move side-to-side,
Like a waltz slowed in time,

or dresses you wear in the daytime,
change to a cotton nightgown caress

at night. When it's me alone and not enough,
I close my eyes and smell coconut.

Beach Rose

A deciduous, woody shrub
dense, and multi-stemmed
grow to a height of five feet
you are beautiful in my sightline

your shoulders held the sand dunes—
an indicator, a metaphor, a display
how native and non-native species
struggle in changing conditions.

How noble, your petite fruit called "hips,"
the leaves like my fading, wrinkly skin.
Your curls held the sweet smelling flowers,
white, pink, or purple, with yellow stamens.

My dear Rosa Rogusa, you picked me
from spiny thorns. You will leave me
deserted when summer ends, finding,
my own way back from the path.

Defining Unnatural, Non-Scientific Thunder Bolts

You were the true miracle,
like a statue that really cries.
No trickery, no snake oil, an impossible
vessel of light for others to translate.

Jesus in the toast or pane of glass
or the mold on the wall you talk to
when you are reaching out
expecting an answer.

May lightning strike down
one time, then again,
because that happens
more often than thought.

The recurring dream you had,
tying a flower to a chuppah,
I had the same, bolted up to stare
at the crucifix hung over a lamp.

Reversing the Rain

When reversing the rain,
the sky is closing,
the desert soaking.
Empty hearts lie in cavities.

Some assembly required,
the lengthy daylight.
The taking of theirs.
The losing of yours.

We collected lost postage stamps.
Knowing nothing of Costa Rica.
Nothing of New Guinea.
No expert on geography.

We're experts on the oceanic,
how the fish emptied
the ocean. The whales
washed away to sea.

Serenity splashing,
rolling over anger,
left on the shore then
tossed in the crests.

Serenity, the tossed boat,
trying to dock,
like the wounded whale
needing a rescue.

Window at the Oceanic Hotel

The beauty of the ocean, caught behind
the windblown diaphanous curtain,
is not missed by optic nerves
or imaging sensor chips.

It's the image for all
in many pictures, this one captured
with exponential universality, silent
as we walk up the wooden stairs.

Shared Bathroom at the Oceanic Hotel

Spider over the sink, in a bathroom
web was a giant—ghost of the past,

where I once crushed spiders in my bare hands,
batted them to the ground, crunched

under my right
Converse High-Top.

My mother told me that spiders were
reincarnated from someone we loved,

a miracle in ways unknown to
grasp...

That span over a sink
is spread two feet across,

Queen in the middle, her
body of work inches above

my sightlines, I'd never noticed
until the day I had to duck.

The Holy Orchestrated

Tracking birds overhead,
Eyes like a conductor's

Baton, movement
Follows the Measure.

They cluster on
Monument's point,

Unflocked circles
Tucked in group.

365,000 Poems Written About You

of which none was very good.
I wasn't mad enough,
so the poems turned to love songs
heard on a radio, sung silent.

Quiet, a vehicle without
an engine cannot hum.
Remember when I used to
sing along with it?

A Sonnet First Seen at
Walnut Street Café
February 2019

That night his lenses found divine, soft eyes
A night her tresses shined view of divine
A bull's eye, or wish, in harkening ties.
Newness of words get placed in time.

Is there a symphony of music for them?
A softened note, played in heads, to strong hearts.
Seduce a wish to strike paper and pen.
A-flustered the words requested in part.

Meeting with him, hated saying goodbye.
Sunday cafe decorated in style.
The words got started hello, then hi
wrapped in coats for tea after driving for miles.

Then tried to share, their days in time
holding her hand, fingers entwine.

The People of Star Island

They are like the barn swallows
circling the area and ground
between the porch and the dock,
crisscrossing and figure eights.

Joining each other in ovals,
then dropping off,
only to have another
fall into the open slot.

It's what we see from the porch,
these events happening.
They circle US, and we circle
even sitting at tables or rocking chairs.

Someone will fly off and then a new energy,
a new person, will enter into the pattern,
bird in, bird out—we are the swallows,
circling, admiring, admired.

Walk Until The Legs Go Numb

Socrates: the unexamined life isn't worth living,
But the examined life makes you want to die!

The light in stars will extinguish,
but moonlight's only reflected

on a stream, the foot bridge
curling over the sound of rushed

water thrusting over stones.
You feel no longer a person

holding a hand as fingers become
sand which runs between yours.

Remember when I built a fire?
I stacked the logs for your warmth,

but cold is everlasting, not like
the smoky smell fading from your coat.

Denouement

We were in Boston, the night the world shut down;
you didn't touch the doors or seats or surfaces on the train,

then stayed away from each other
for forty-some-odd days, carefully

keeping distance, until we
risked a kiss in your kitchen.

Acted cautious some more, (I shopped at 6 AM.
You yelled at your father for going to Home Depot)

so that COVID only existed in others,
not on chances taken by us.

Committed to Wednesdays and Saturdays
saved for each other: cooked, streamed,

played music: guitar, ukulele, and
called it our band; harmony sounded good.

Music, and books were trusted gifts I sent.
Clearly, you said, *I had a big heart.*

Found an oasis, with the trips we took
three hours West, to disappear at an Inn.

It was our place: We climbed Greylock,
ate Mexican, sat in a Jacuzzi with battery-lit candles.

The after touched hands on silk, smooth, warm,
our damp bodies under sheets and bed's canopy.

We made love like mad people
until disentanglement of arms and legs.

Then, we stopped at a farm stand on the way back
which gave us the best pickles we ever tasted.

It was the stuff you did,
not said, the actions:

When my father died you brought bags of food
which were exactly the same as when Mom passed,

then after, realizing how life was less,
I brought you a broken guitar,

so you could smash it on the sidewalk, but
it still sits in one piece, respecting the instrument.

And, the last time at the Inn, I walked
into a table and the glass shattered.

When you cooked for me last, the egg cracked
rotten into the dessert you were making,

but it was me making greater blunders:
clearly, you said, *I use bad judgment,*

leaving me a last amend: one for loving you,
then sobbing at the table at the Border Café,

and still afterward in the parking lot
as it rained, my shoulders heaved,

wishing I'd held it together, as I tried
to keep them from falling off.

Addictions

Political puppets are real,
vices defined by party line *and lines...*

Note: now cookie monster gives out apple slices,
which is not bad until someone says, cookies are crack.

Note: the way words are thrown around
as if they have meaning, importance.

Note: we are all very important, said by
the crusted, treasonable citizens.

Note: this is our house, join us,
please, march with us,

our tight muscles trudging, the skin
a snare drum struck with brutal force.

Note: let's do some trekking in time
like lyrical spaghetti thrown on a tile.

Note: I hate to needle you but
replace all ceramic behind your stovetop.

Note: words are our only epiphanies, "hello, hi,
higher ground," get up, get up, get up.

At the Farm in Elkton, Maryland

In Memory of Jones Purcell

You will go down this dark road,
not seeing the gaps in the barn plank.

And the starry sky is layered Picasso,
as if it's seen in black and white.

And every October the mice
have decided to move inside,

the smell is of fireplace
and smoked whiskey, old

newspaper blanketing the sofa
to cover where the dog peed.

Living room decorated in
guitars—amps, and cords

dancing over wood floors, creating
Venn diagramed dirt within circles.

Glassfuls of bourbon will create songs
as you yell, "I am not to go anywhere

until we have three of four of them!
Here's a pen; write something to this!"

Dog On Zoom

Dog on the floor.
Dog on the wall.
Dog pictured in.
Your zoom square.
Does anyone detect
It's you, your dog,
Sharing the room with
Me, You, Dog,
All of it, a secret.

COVID Fears

Of being found in decomposition
on a hot day, body into soup.

The thin walls, a barrier for the obvious
Acridity, but clearly heard is the constant

sound of a neighbor's television
or their marches up the stairs.

If we go missing without being
looked in on—we never existed

more than that tiny speck of dust
waving in the sun on the nightstand.

Even exhales within the silence
of a forest hike can be seen,

even when it's just you pausing
to see the same old trees,

realizing you have walked in circles,
then inhaling the cold, cold sense of void.

Listen in order to hear your god say:
Pal. This is where you are welcome.

Deductions and Ends

The sawdust floor of The Dirtier Bar
is crescent-shaped in its swirls,

created by my sneaker when
I slipped off to use the john,

sure to not step on a foot
of a Pagan member, who stab

people for less than some sideways look
or a cut in line as they waited for their beers

in a crowd arced three-deep from
the tap and long, glossed mahogany.

The Suicidiversary: Years and A Day Late

I don't know where
his family is now—
parents, a sister, his brothers,
Steven and...
Dave, that's his name,
lives here somewhere
in Massachusetts, I can't remember

the town, like many old memories,
good or bad, shuffled in my head.
Happy Anniversary, I cried,
yesterday, was just a Wednesday.
Yesterday a day where I could feel the knife
jousting his wrist the way it did,
as a stabscotch within my thoughts.

30 years later,
the cut, deep to the wrist,
bleeds out angrily, still,
I no longer really remember
the exact time. Was it 31 years or 29?
I can't calculate. I've forgotten how—
I have forgotten a lot, not just that.

Opposite Magnetic Poles

Spring's rain burst upon your
face, slapping down the plastic sheet
film of water sliding down,
drop by drop,
holding your breath;
the thunder, and lightning

left one another like a leaked secret,
without holding any brightness
within the darkest skies, while
the room continues to flash
the unfurled art made
from Summer's naked forms.

In July the trees hold tight
to green leaves, taking Autumn
for granted, yellow leaves
form from cold air, then red,
until brown appears...
causing you to die inside.

Fewer hours and that's as depressing as
my death cracking under my Pumas.
The tilt in the shoe matching
how the earth's axis spins
in exaggeration of time passing.
If only you could see just today,

that robin early,
in February,
on a chain link fence,
immediately flying off,
Dear, dear, robin. Cold,
into the dead of Winter.

Dinner Party

The kitchen's horde sits or stands
configured as serpentine shapes.

Stove sending warmth seen as steam-willows,
while the hostess offers her stirring spoon

to strange lips, mixing the hallowed hellos,
with all the ones forbidden to each.

One waiting, to present the
creation, folded in, as a fabric,

the downing of drinks,
welcomed reverie, the bar

ever as close, the countertop,
the clientele askew on stools.

Conclusive consensus quoted in chorus,
"The kitchen is where folks congregate."

Good, as the hullabaloo
caused the holdup in dinner,

while her lucky dog nuzzles,
noses in, nothing but contentment,

therapeutically weaving within
a colliding kaleidoscope of limbs,

like a figure skater gliding,
fourth in beguiling figures of eight.

Streaming While Napping

Wrestler Dave Schultz was shot
by a du Pont with a gun.

Fox catcher wrestled with
gun violence, mental health.

Pet rabbit's ears up, they sit on the carpet.
TV is on. They are apathetic, while I nap.

A #nap, waken to find the army
created new guidelines

after Vanessa Guillen died.
20/20-ABC #IamVanessaGuillen.

When someone is murdered
somethings gotta be done about it.

Eyes closed to another Social Dilemma
I've woken up to the same old story.

Crap, I have to rewind
to the John du Pont episode,

the team paid his opponents off
so he believed he had won.

Global Conditions

It's rained every day in July,
August too.
June, May, October.
Rained the entire year.

Unless, it was snow
or fog instead,
much in the head of
those in the world.

Sump pumps will blow up, our
shoulders now bigger from shoveling,
we can no longer lift fog
or rain or push by plow.

The water will rise and rise
from melting, expanding
temperatures. We are melting
clouds, the pies in the sky.

So, Look up!
It is Falling!
I refuse to play Chicken,
Dammit! It *is* falling.

Seasonal Fire Effect

Thoughts on The Bootleg Fire

The sky, black,
the timbre of cinder—
cinder of ash
in time.

To scientists, listen:
New atmospheric fear,
fears of a billion degrees
of heat.

Or don't. It's optional.
Fiction is daft fact:
facts are feelings
you tweet.

Disregard others as:
Greta is a shrill pill.
Pills are not a hobby,
like a boyfriend,

in Winter inside the
forgetful flogging fire log:
logs crumble as frozen
spikes form.

Snap and give up, don't overlook
nor remember embers wild:
wild to remember long warnings
effacing a thought.

Thoughts over the Deluge

I'd driven blind through many,
the odds this time of surviving

with one eye closed,
the other fading to half-staff...

If you stare sideways at the world
it blurs together out the side window;

the trick is to quit
before ejected from this

scene, the saturation
will easily break the fall.

Science

It's a two-sided conclusion.
Those exhilarating experiments
kept you up all night burning,
approving the science of fire.

Questions answered about color
depended on temperature.
Chemical reactions take the credit
for ignition of fuel and oxygen.

Atoms rearranged themselves forever.
Combustion will continue
fuel, heat, and oxygen,
resulting in hues.

Ever see a blue flame of high oxygen?
Reaction between carbon and hydrogen
produces blue and violet,
its flames are the hottest.

Reds were cool, and lighter
scorching temperatures.
The fierce orange is due to sodium,
lithium turned to red.

Always defeated by white flame,
which we cannot forget.
White flames leads to
everything coming together.

Political Climate

Close the door,
which is difficult when swollen.
Paint is forced off the wood,
catches, until slammed,
louder than intended.
Intolerable—to stay cool,
when the Mercury rages
angry in a state of red.

Occupy Forever

For Blaine Hebbel

Protesters continue their action;
the American Voices captured,

laconic words factored—
the lengthy rants rapture.

When activists occupied Dewey Square
those days you left your mark there,

never silenced into muck
by police or garbage trucks.

The occupoets organized
rhymes, reasons, against lies,

shouted out in today's times:
truth for all, still hard to find.

Counting the rings within your bones,
the careful aging of factual tones,

like the music which permeates your poems,
has a chance far better than the lone

few percent rates, versus the other 98, because
people calibrate—that's for damn straight.

What Dante Learned

One sin is enough of a mistake
you cannot try to make

again. You are charred by
the torture within yourself,

that special place in hell.
Dark. Dismal. Demented.

The world as an illusion means nothing.
Something cannot be something else.

Spare ye such pain à la Beatrice,
who arrived too late, such a non-lesson

St. Lucia seemed
to prompt her along.

And the Simonists, you scold,
will learn or burn. The takeaway:

you are exactly where
you are supposed to be, Lucifer,

your insurgence squashed
by the many scholarly souls.

Introduction to a Séance at Turning Tables: Delphine de Girardin for Victor Hugo

The peak is my catacomb.
I am lungs full of Spirit,
God the air we inhale;

chests rise and drop off
wanting to be in Earth's ether,
but the dirt asked me back.

I am pulled to where there were
collisions with the Sagittarius Dwarf,
casket spikes latching on and cut.

The dark tugs toward "hell,"
the light to "rapture."
Melancholy, the possibility,

watching countless graves
peer into the skulls after decomposition.
I am now the initiator of nightmares.

The Great Appearing Act

Some innovative perception
Love perspective
Life lights
Life lines
Show on expressions.

In moments of reprieve
hope, in moments of dismissal
Life lights
Most fire
Terrible of the elements.

Bypass the bird struck,
Feathers in a breakdown lane
Life lights
Depend upon
Changing the way

Of magic, the only science
Unaccepted by graceful
Life lights
Exploding through darkness
We are honored to reveal.

Not Perfect Does Not Make Practice

There's the time she pulled into the garage
she'd entered thousands of times,
this time hitting the back wall.
The wall to face repairs,
the car also in need—

to take me to the gym,
"Don't talk about *practice*,"
my mother said,
dry lips like plaster,
and broken-eyed vessels,

I kept my arms length from the car,
sundown till darkness,
until practice was over.
Cracked wall left crumbles on hood,
but skewed headlights stayed on.

Mutualism

I don't know when we stopped.
You being an oxpecker, me a zebra,

or a bee and a flower,
or a spider crab with algae.

Human intestine and resident bacteria.
Ocean anemone, and god. Was I a clownfish?

Yet, we sometimes cooperative, never mycorrhizal
we never became completely deep rooted...

But it woke a monster inside me;
now watch phylogenetics in action.

Watch a being mammothly throw me
like the backwards sea, never alone

without the us in us, we
in the we—apparent predation.

A beast gets reintroduced,
a salty symbiotic creature,

a parasite from my past, watching
how you barely hang on.

In The Obituary of Paul Felopulos

The hero turned a lifeboat around,
when the in-charge maître d's order of rowing
toward the Prisendam were unsound.

At eighteen he took over, crowned
himself captain, no experience of knowing
ship suction, commanded the rowboat around.

Back at two AM the alarm sounded,
Rousted him up, the tasks began growing
engine on fire, the sinking ship now unsound.

Fifty people would jam a 28-seat boat, sent pulley downed.
Passenger's unruly panic continued ongoing.
Yet the calm teen captain has not been around

25-foot waves, against a tiny boat pounded
for days and days, their crests curled bowing.
But no one now felt his leadership unsound.

Then two days later, rescue helicopters. Hopes abound!
Taking charge again, the survivors impatient in going.
You controlled the uncontrollable rescue around.

Two days after, everyone was safe aground.
No less, life expectances reduced nor slowing.
Paulie, the hero, neither a word here unsound.
He never told me this story while he was around.

The Haunted Mile

People share their workouts
in the same way they tell you
what medications they're on.

They talk as if they know you.
If only they didn't,
they would want to

know that everything is fine
(frantic-insane
-nuts-egotistical).

When the speakers leave their homes
they are running *from*—because
running *to* something—is the finish.

Vaccination Extravaganza

At the circus, performed a one-pony trick,
round and round Center Ring, horse and rider dazzled.
At one point, she stood on her head, not using
arms or legs for extra support—oh, and she spun

like a gyroscope. I checked my glasses
to make sure I wasn't seeing things.
Because I can see everything!
I made mountains out of molehills,

OR (*as we know, we have choices,*
and understand things, even without therapy)
molehills out of mountains
(*depending on the day*).

But, logic is circular, and that's when she went
horse-back-revolving, witnesses riveted
on their many-times-over-painted seats.
Will she fall? We watched. We couldn't not

watch her. Then applause
for the Ringmaster,
waving his hyperbole, so...
we can now all breathe.

It Happens in Spring

when everything blooms—
the green, the buds, the blossoms,

despite popular belief, thoughts
blacker than the previous season.

When snow falls in April,
that's not at all backwards.

It's the cruelty Eliot wrote about rebirth
as a desolate emotional landscape,

when the warmer weather activates,
ignites the fervor for self-destruction.

The added drain of collaborating contact
Durkheim directly depicted—

the potent disappointment as
Winter is overtaken by Spring,

light becoming dark.
The dark heads to light.

The Attenuation of
Wide Ranges of Thoughts

Will the cables on the bridge snap?
How far will the car drop before it hits water?
One one-thousand, two-one-thousand?
What will you think in that time of ailing? Life is so short?

While driving on any large bridge
you think of that, when noticing blotches
of rust on girders, the need for paint
is just a sign-post hiding other unheeded
faults of structures, like tunnels, roads,

mental notes
affect-relationships

about sink holes and dust storms, wildfires, cancers
and viruses. The people on the street that will rob you
of your dignity, the guy in the tree when you were a child
in bed, terrified nightly, but he was never there.

People went to work on 9-11, the tower's
long arms stretched to heaven,
before and after, no one knew
things beyond our control can kill you,
then it's too late, always too late, to be too late.

Sanity is the cables, steel, and concrete
whose bridges falter under cars.
The visions in your head, never stationary
solid rock. Schemata is our torture.

Somnambulism

I slept-walked
Benadryl ate
pizza

drank
Red Bull
woke

willy-walked
back to
bed

restless
wrestled
sheet

Nighthawks

Not found on counter juke box,
just like her hand is unplayable

when reached for tonight,
the way he's reached for it forever.

The waiter is the cook, is the host,
the coffeemaker, the bill collector

chasing the man right now for an order,
while she's been caught in an indifferent

evening out, now a stalled conversation.
The man asks, "What do you want?"

as an uncomfortable stranger at the counter
becomes worth his weight in avoiding eye-contact.

No one answers any questions,
not about the pie, which are too easy,

baked today: cherry or apple;
blueberry was yesterday.

She answers she no longer likes blueberry,
or the diner, or the Special, certainly not the Special.

There Once Was a Harvest

Red pickup sat in the track of dried mud,
in desolation, as death left you alone,
rust around the body and bed,
tired dirt sprayed on its rubber.
Parked near a barn once glossed
in a thick corona blue,
distressed, peeling, the color
fights a battle with the barn board.

A yellow piece of fabric blows
through this hacked-out yard
the man with scythed-cut hair
pitches up his gaze for miles-
-around-miles in all-ways direction.
The sun-singed corn stands at attention
straight and stiff, its kernels burned and drying
husks wave slightly, offering him nothing.

Ode to a Tree Cut Down

You can no longer grow. Your roots bore into pipe
below a basic foundation under my neighbor's house.
They watched each branch cut, streamlined, and then saw
rope used to pull you down, as if you were nothing.

I will stand with you tree, protest going down.
Hope the structure can plumb itself,
become an element of change,
not just leafed branches severed,

raining down your splendor,
becoming dank down
to your trunk; appendages exposed,
cut up, taken away, forgotten.

Can I Fly You a Drink?

*A found poem from an internet article
with internet comments*

A waxwing eats a berry from an arrowwood tree.
Birds are known to gorge on fermented fruit.
Life lately in tiny Gilbert, Minnesota,
resembles a scene out of a Hitchcock movie.

The residents call 911:
Rowdy birds fly into
windows and cars,
acting confused.

Cops conclude the unruly birds
are not out for blood,
just had too many...
They'll feel bad in the morning.

And having a boozy lark is nothing
abnormal in the feathered set,
a line between tipsy or fall-down drunk
is picked out correctly every now and then.

No need to call emergency services
to report inebriated avians: they'll sober up shortly.
No crime in flying home with someone
you normally wouldn't nest with, just shame.

How to Be a Werewolf

Perhaps just a simple pact
with the Devil or a curse from a God
(see Lycaon and Zeus),
but since He no longer curses,

leave it to witches
in a deliberate act
of hoo-doo voo-doo,
if that's the way you spell it.

And around the South American short tail
the Lobis-homem—Great balls of fire!

But, certainly not a universal picture, except
in Hollywood, from a bite from the wolf
who bit two friends who bit two more
and so on, and so on, and so on and so on.

Not lycanthropy, in which one is convinced
by their mind they are non-human
shape shifters forming into wolves,
but that's just crazy...and...

not to flood you with excess syndromes
like hypertrichosis unrelated to the hair of the dog
though Barnum's boy Jojo, born with that face, that face,
wasn't a werewolf—only a sideshow, according to PT.

Which leaves it to the werewolves,
requiring one or more of the parents
being werewolves—lucky them;
to be born that way.

Family Silence for Sixty-Two Years

I remember mother's fury after her silence
from an innocuous question my father answered.

"Mom, what is your mother's maiden name?"
Acted as if Angelo LaMarca had answered it himself.

We stared into the empty fireplace;
the entire house is going up and up and up.

It *could* happen in the suburbs of Long Island,
you *could* leave an infant sleeping outdoors,

not worry about anything or anyone,
not even a taxi-driver, Angelo,

who would write a ransom note
implying threats and apologies.

Don't tell anyone,
I'm watching you.

I'm sorry.
I'm in bad need of money.

Two-thousand. In small bills.
I'm scared stiff. One false move and...

Signed,
The babysitter

Then he missed the first drop-off exchange,
then missed two more, never showed up.

I am frightened of the press, he wrote,
another note where to find the Weinberger baby.

Found
d e a d.

My mother would never ever talk about it.
My grandmother had never spoken about it.

But my father responded only with a last name,
during a family vacation, at a city by the sea,

a first cousin twice removed,
never could be removed enough.

Frosting On a Barren Field

Brown panels under splattered white
tufts of snow, blue sky panoramic chamber,
the gear stuck in overdrive.

Fifty-five seems like zero. You are
slight against the scene. The heater
cranks, car shields and protects .

Your naked soul could crack
like thin ice on the edges of the road.
There you are, sitting small in all that.

Inlet Sunset

"Row," you say,
"row."

as the last pulls are rainbow
droplets off the oar.

The sunset off Rehoboth Bay
enflames the marsh's tall grass.

It tints McKinley Street, as we walk
to the cove where Chuck, a name

for your father, and "asshole"
for your brother- are a-driftin'.

Chuck is working on the motor,
agitated now. The engine is still.

Chuck curses, smoking, because,
"the goddamn thing won't catch!"

They are pulled farther out. They can't hear
you say it, but they begin to row.

We Are the Ones Left on the Beach

For Natalie

When we view the sunset,
we will view our own hues
because the light of you, Natalie,
make the colors different today.

To us who pass here nightly,
the tinges of orange, blue,
yellow, and red, do not burst into conflict
when blooming without you
as you bloomed for us daily.

The beach is no longer your beach;
we will never go back to being
what we were before the thrush
of cold, when those incoming storms
are the aural of your voice.

God and You

1.

The first time I was ever
in the higher power of God,
not running my own life, I thought
Maya Angelou never needed
anyone in charge,
she just needed to turn the page.
I was on my knees then;

I closed my mind
immediately and hard.
I've got, and I needed,
really-really-really needed,
an outside perspective
to know what's the best for me.

When I worked on the farm,
God was supposed to do that.
He did nothing but make me laugh.
That's not a good God. I was reminded
that I saved a three letter name
beginning with G for a day I could use it.

2.

Take a trip if you want to come up
to celebrate 6 AM.
It's been 20 years since
we stayed in Yellowstone,
and, yeah, I'm still struggling:
maybe nine months-six months-three months.

One month is when you're coming?
I love you even with *that* mouth.
Can you hear me at this distance
saying, *I don't need people*
I can stay in my room.
But I don't have to be that person anymore.

And I don't even think I'll be saved
when droplets from a waterfall
are no longer music at 6 AM,
observing the heights and depths
of a prayer at a geyser.
What else is here but that?

Tuumaq

When God's cold hands
lose their grip, the moon falls off
like a crooked ship, and trees reach
as broken ladders beg. Will the

Father find his way back
to prove productive
after being abandoned
at night while he slept?

The ocean feeds itself
on melted sheaths;
a death so complicated
it cannot be just one word:

"Senilicide, Invalidicide,"
if adopted under extreme conditions,
seems grotesque to others,
rarely practiced during times of worth.

There is no evidence
of anyone sent out
on an ice float being relaxed.
A logistically difficult task,

to create something cracked
away from a seaside;
the risk of breaking off
their final chapter in mistake.

Yet, snow can be
ganek, kaneq, nutaryuk, pirta, qengaruk̦
but they're really only descriptors.
for snow—abstract lexemes are human.

Christmas 2019

Stunned awake by ring tone
—nothing good comes of—that

nurse asking if you'd like
to say a final goodbye

as your mother lies dying in a hospice bed.
Maybe they're only keeping her alive

so you can drive to Harbor House at
midnight, because hospice is respectful

the same way a neighbor will
later send you a sympathy card.

So, you tell the nurse, No
because you have said

goodbye every day
for the past two months,

sat there at the bedside, heard
her whisper she wasn't scared

of what comes after. She said,
you know, one time,

she smelled the scent
of roses in the dead of Winter.

Never Heard at Home

My father used to say *Howdy,*
but only while on vacation.

Howdy, as if he were greeting
a friendly cowboy on the range.

Still the out-of-place greeting
tailed off in a faint question mark,

perhaps self-realizing that he's a quiet man,
never greeted anyone in day-to-day life.

Who was this man,
who struggled at home

with words, with never even a *Hi,*
or *Howdy* for any of us???

Or in conversation
started...stuttered...but

what exactly could he speak about
at dinner? Nothing about his job,

building radar systems which
tracked nuclear warheads

during the Cold War, as the quiet
steam rose from the mashed potatoes.

Then on vacation, he greeted all
Howdy, and "Hello," they said back.

patents held by charles h. gager
and charles fowler
(Apparatus for double cancellation utilizing one delay line in a moving target indicating system-1959)

Let's see if I got this per my limitations in defense intelligence.

Discriminating between mixed and moving objects or between moving objects at different speeds using transmissions or interrupted pulse modulated waves based up the phase or frequency shift resulting from movement of objects, with reference to the transmitted signals.

Which Means? (if viewed as a radar screen below):

            let's   see
       my father   worked on
       radar   defense
   so this invention   hmmm, is about
radar, or a pulse radar,   telling the defense engineer

how fast, or even if   **Θ**   an object (a missile),

is a moving TARGET,   ...and quickly.
  So based on   picking up on
    the signals of this   object, this missile,
      this weapon of   mass destruction:

CLAIMS:

a double cancellation circuit for moving-target indicating systems comprising: a carrier oscillator; means coupled to said carrier oscillator for amplitude-modulating the output of said carrier oscillator with recurrent pulses; means coupled to said amplitude-modulating means for detecting the amplitude difference between successive pulses of said recurrent pulses; means coupled to said amplitude difference detecting means for phase modulating the output of said carrier oscillator with the output of said difference detector; and means coupled to said phase-modulating means for detecting the phase difference of successive pulses of said recurrent pulses.

Which Means?

OK, I think I got it.

That's the machine itself.

Let's see if I got this per my limitations in knowledge about my father: Radar Engineer, worked on Star Wars Defense System.

Hmmm...a couple of nuclear missiles being developed in the late 1950s.

So,
wait. I
got it: This
patent is to
detect attacking
missiles so we
can blow them
out of the air
before they
kill us. Kill
them before

they fucking
kill us.

filed june 4, 1959 coherent vldeo input-w
reactance tube frequency modulator carrier oscillator normal video
input-and limiter frequency discriminator delayed coherent video
output amplitude detector delayed normal video output inventors,

charles a. fowler charles h. gager.
CLASSIFIED

Father's Day/Funeral

What can do you do
Five days after his service

Celebrating life
Sharing his passing

June 14, we placed his ashes,
Father's Day came quickly that Sunday

I had no one to call
This year, I did not forget him

Curled into the arm of an arm chair
Weak as an embryo

Sleep, My Dear Poets

Far greater than silencing
the sound of your words.

Write this: a mother's cancer
is not a word on a page.

A father going peacefully
doesn't deserve any stanzas.

Wanting to take their pills,
the first one makes you sleepy.

Millions and millions of people
have slept from a virus. Sleep,

you anonymous targets of active shooters.
I know, dear poet, you are sorry.

then, die before you write a single goddam word,
write now, write now, write never, write forever.

Jones' Song

Just a shadow in a moonlit
circle hastened to domed fit.

Was that Jones
up on the trestle,

guitar slung on back,
standing crooked on the track?

This friend of mine,
the October sky.

He wrote that having love was
climbing a mount-top, then shoved

off a cliff, perhaps, he
thought-he-must-a slipped.

The thousand nuns prayed
for the lost souls of that trip,

praying for you,
        praying for you,
                        their

hymns serenade you tight
on the big, black-inked night.

Living with Rabbits

I speak
to rabbits in
quarantine, or no one
else in the world.

Today, I sing to them
about what they are doing
with their lives, as they sleep
and munch hay into mulch.

The rabbits boast long back legs,
quite strong. They leap forward
great distances with a single push.
They move quick—in short bursts,

good for leaping into the air or
forward over the ground,
when out of their cages.
I relate to this happiness.

Rarely, I feel that free.

I am Alone

(Watching bad movies during the Pandemic)
after the movie Fathers and Daughters *(Warning Spoiler Alert)*

A little girl can't be nicknamed Potato Chip
Then as a grown woman,
still be called Potato Chip.

And a man can't start a seizure, hold it off,
walk to the bathroom, then flop involuntarily.
Seizures do not work that way.

For that matter, neither does
getting psychiatrically institutionalized
for seizure disorder for seven months

and upon returning for
young daughter, Potato Chip,
brother and sister-in-law suggest keeping her

because they really love her,
and epilepsy equals incompetence,
plus their boys and Potato Chip really get along,

which leads to future pushing
and father punching brother-in-law
who is, by the way, a lawyer

now presenting a custody suit
which doesn't matter.
He had an affair.

His secretary is now pregnant
also, moot point because father
dies seizing on the bathroom floor.

Meanwhile...
we never find out if Potato Chip
was brought up by the sister-in-law.

But now grown up Potato Chip—
she has meaningless,
unfeeling sex all over New York City

until she meets
Aaron Paul who I wrestled with not being
Jesse Pinkman or Todd from Bojack

who read the father's book,
Fathers and Daughters,
then calls her Potato Chip too!

He loves her, and she loves him,
but she *just can't* and has meaningless, unfeeling
sex all over New York City.

Aaron Paul expected more because
Potato Chip is a working therapist
who helped a traumatized girl to speak again.

If only
my damn living room could talk,
it would tell me

there is no possible way Potato Chip
can jog to Jesse or Todd or whomever's
house sometime in daylight,

arriving way after dark. And,
of course, he is with a woman,
so she literally runs home back,
.

losing the long running and crying marathon
because, lo' and behold, Jesse or Todd had a car,
beating her, already parked outside her house.

They hug.

The End.

Things I May Say Which Annoy People

The monarchs in the loo
were flushing queens.

When butterflies, will
they change to margarine?

The raw idea for a muffin
was only half baked.

I sprayed Pledge outside
for dusting the wind.

I shoveled dirt to bury my ashes,
and made a perfect ash-hole!

I ate a Burpee seed
then repeated myself, once more,

When I remembered a writing buddy
who turned out to be a palomine.

How to Revise a Poem

Read lightly the first time through.
Then read it, again, lightly.
Then read it a third time, this time aloud
(if you haven't already tried it that way).
Note places that sound clunkity-clunk.*
Set it down.
Look out your window,
if one is handy.
If one is not,
look at your foot,
or hand, or your lunch.
Then pick up a pen
(a fountain pen if you own one)
write words which come to mind
related to lines you actually like.
Do this for a while.
Then return to entire poem.
Read lightly.
Consider something new.

*use this line for an example.

Secrets and Compartments

"The tissue box lies crushed in the back seat
of the Subaru my father used to drive."
~ New flash fictions, 2019-2022

Nor'easter

"The weather is incredible," Rebecca said as black sheets of rain pelted the windows and sidewalks outside of The Halloween Boo-Boo Store in Salem, Massachusetts. Rebecca had been working twenty-one straight days in October with or without any available stock. They kept running out of the half-sized witch's hats the mask-less tourists loved so much. Sunny and seventy degrees drew the tourists in like zombies in search of brains.

"The town has come to celebrate innocent women being put to death," Rebecca slurred at her husband before she passed out at 10 PM, eight hours of sleep buried by dreams of rock slides trapping coal miners in Appalachia. She thought she heard him agree, and Rebecca loved that he supported her unconditionally, especially when she'd quit her nursing job and headed over to retail. "Too much sadness, the sick, the dying, the virus."

Now she had to deal with the fudge and sweets that the factory needed to whip up before they were pillaged by customers who wanted to buy something, or anything, as with tourists, they just needed to buy something, or anything. It was difficult to keep up with them. She wanted to test the consumerism of the tourists, so Rebecca had asked her boss if they could package the delicious fudge as Hester Prynne's feces. He just looked at her as if she hadn't lived in Salem for her entire life.

So the rain came, and not even the umbrellas showed up, none of them forced to be turned inside out. Rebecca thought that the goodies she put out would sell more if people claimed that a spell was put on them. Then she went through the list of spells she knew, which included cyanide and molly, and stirred some killer nuts into the fudge, hoping that she didn't have to explain cross-contamination to anyone today.

The Kicker Loses the Game

He is a kicker. Not really a player, but someone needed to do what he is paid to do when it's all on the line. He doesn't tackle, run, or throw—only kicks a large, inflated slug ten feet above the ground, within a spread of 18.5 feet from various distances depending, on where the football players leave him.

His girlfriend doesn't understand football. She says it's just a bunch of guys crashing into one another. It's what he likes about her. The kicker actually thinks the same thing. He likes to point out those things they have in common. He, of course, is more civilized, his job more of an engineer than a pugilist.

He thinks his teammates like him, but they are noncommittal. Sure a kicker has benefits worth a few points, but he's not really like them. She thinks the same, but has a tough time explaining to her friends and her parents who he is, *"Um, yes, he's a football player, but he's just the kicker."*

One week the kicker misses, so she lets him go. He wants a hug, but she's a waver, watching from the yard as he walks away. She creeps the videos he posts on Instagram too soon after his release: the kicker sprinting forty yards...the kicker throwing the ball through the hole of a hung steel-belted radial...the kicker, hitting a tackling dummy.

Late Night TV Ad, Summer 2020

Tired of sitting at home, waiting for the government to tell you when you can leave your home and when you can't? Tired of the medical professionals not finding a cure for Covid-19, which is imprisoning us? Tired of your own medical and psychiatric diagnosis surging and growing, costing thousands and thousands of dollars to treat? Well, gather round your zoom screens, because I have the cure you are looking for.

You have spent or you will spend thousands looking for relief from this, but now, for nearly less than a third of the price to treat you, let me, Doc Clark, virtually get you out of your house and into the real world! Who knows, maybe you will be earning like you've never earned before, becoming one of those highly paid social influencers.

You've all heard that this quarantine will be going on for years, and the depression, the isolation, is about as bad the virus itself. You've said to yourself, this is a terrible period in everybody's lifetime. Well, let me show you what I can do for you! Before I do that, let me remind you of someone. Remember 78-year-old Kate Stanley? Mrs. Stanley was stuck at home, much like you are, without the ability to see her adult children, or her grandchildren. Not allowed to leave her home, with no one allowed to enter, Mrs. Stanley contacted me, Doc Clark, and her life went viral. You all remember her as Granny Mountain Climber, conquering Mount Everest. In fact, I have a number for you. Sixty-three percent of you gave her a virtual clap from home, and from the safe comfort of your Internet. Best of all, she had social contact.

How about this guy? You remember Nolan Abraham's walk up the Red Carpet, on Oscar Night, with Selena Gomez hooked on his arm? After accepting the award for Best Actor, in a movie none of you had ever seen? And, of course, none of you have seen it, because no one is leaving their homes...but...in his acceptance speech, guess who he names? That's right, me, Doc Clark.

Now, as you sit in your sad, depressed living room, are you wondering how Granny Mountain Climber, and Academy Award winner Nolan Abraham are out in the real world and succeeding? Here's the catch: They are not!

But now, you too can become a success the same way they did. For just $9,999 dollars, I will become your agent. As your real licensed agent, you will get my services, for not a penny more than the agreed $9,999. I promise to get you out of your house and into the homes of the rest of the world successfully. Now you might be saying, "This is unsafe," or, "How can I leave my home without getting sick?" Some of you are worried that if you are seen in public, you may be charged with manslaughter for helping spread Covid-19, for which we are in isolation. Well, I'm here to tell you that there is no risk, no gimmick in any of this. If you buy the *Gold Medal Celebrity Package*, I, Doc Clark, will integrate you digitally into any person, place, or thing, you want, whether it's a movie star, a well-known athlete, or a billionaire with power. That's right, you can be whatever you want. And remember this isn't a one-time thing. We will continue to promote and place your new outside life all over the Internet, such as on news outlets, social media, prime-time specials, and ABC After Virtual School Specials-all of them, so that you will be exactly at the very top of a regular normal society, conceived the way it used to be!

Maybe being a star in Hollywood, or a Super Bowl Champion is not your cup of tea. Perhaps your friends will recognize that you don't look good enough or athletic enough to be in those roles. Well don't be left in your living room, because we also can get you out of the house with our *Special Success Package.* With this, and for less than the *Gold Medal Celebrity Package,* you can be a successful businessman, drive a nice car, have a lovely house, be married, and be seen vacationing with a lovely, attractive woman that any man would desire. We can get your picture on all these covers: *Business Weekly, Parade,* or even *People* magazine, and you, while sitting at home, will be vibrant, visible, and have a life second-to-none, displayed for all to see in the very depressing world of their loneliness. We can garner you all of this success for a very low price of $3,499.

But, wait! Not looking to go that far? Want to stay famous while still remaining humble? Well there's the *Five Minutes of Fame Package,* which will guarantee you strong hits on social media for at least nine-months, or the same amount of time it takes to bring you into the next baby boom! Again, we will digitally place you in a funny situation, such as a scene with a cute cat, committing an embarrassing but endearing faux-pas, or any other viral-inducing act. You will be Internet notorious, certainly not someone locked indoors saying, "Poor me." Get those nine months of Internet celebrity treatment all for $999.

Now, remember our goal is to break you out of your own seclusion to become the envy of every other isolator in the world. If you act now, we will place you on a brand new social media platform, developed by me, Doc Clark, which will be sure to be the next big thing. It'll be called Clark Bar, and you will be one of the very first influencers on it. Send payment now by Venmo, Paypal, Apple Pay, or a credit card directly to me, Doc Clark, a real licensed agent, and you will start today!

Rabbit Care

It was the kind of fair I was never allowed as a child. *Too crowded, too expensive, too dangerous, and much too much trouble to get there.* Now, as an adult, I came here, and I was leaving with a rabbit. It was a rabbit, housed in a metal cage, with four other rabbits, where children would shriek and poke at them every night. I admired the woman who handed her over to me. "Thanks," I said.

I hadn't come to the fair alone, nor now was I leaving that way. I had left the people I came with- they were all too gleeful, running to The Devil's Wheel, The Hurricane, and the Kamikaze. Fuck, if they raced each other to the kiddie rides. They were in their fifties, but they were crazy like children. I concluded long ago that I was crazy myself, and a crazy person cannot objectively judge such things as others' sanity.

The first few rides were enough for me to want to go home. It was the Star Flyer swing, which rose up into the frigid autumn air and raced you like the wind until tears poured out of you like an open faucet. The second ride jostled me so much, that when I got off the ride, I had a flashback which took me to the side of a road, walking away from a wreck, needing to be rescued.

I found that others needing to be rescued usually lived rough lives, and in a way, were the ones who were always allowed to attend fairs such as this as kids, without missing a year, when it was in town. This rescue rabbit cost twenty-five dollars, bought from a girl with wide cut openings on the side of her loose Metallica tee-shirt, which, opened her up for a lot of comments, yet strangely my admiration was not sexual. It was how she wore the shirt, in her I-don't-give-a-fuck kind of way that gave her an air of complete confidence. It was her body, her strength regarding what was hers, that I admired, so I kept looking at her and shut my fucking mouth as she took my money, gave me a cardboard carrier and a few pieces of paper about rabbit care.

She Does (Doesn't) Exist

A dream featuring someone I've never met, or heard of, but who actually exists.

I was at an art gallery. This person was the central character in all the paintings, drawings, etchings. A character with Cheshire teeth. Her mother, the artist, drew her, painted her, etched her.

There she sat, on the window sill. I recognized her mouth. We talked as if we've known each other for years. "I have some other lovers and am involved in a light affair," she tells me. Her teeth were beautiful.

I tell my own mother I've just met the woman in the paintings, the drawings, the etchings. In my dream, I know her name. No one has names in my dreams. I don't remember them, and I don't remember my dreams.

And we became lovers and rode the Ferris Wheel before she ran off in the dust of the fairgrounds: the was sun sliding down but hadn't disappeared yet.

The Training of Staff

"Please, worker? Be kind to my father."

I try to be as nice as possible to dirty-scrubs Sam, as it might have some benefit. It's not karma, rather an equation: good going out produces good coming in. Either way, it's more the chance he may favor my father in the future if I am nice. Maybe he will help him find his glasses or make a phone call. Maybe he won't steal clothes he knows would look great on him.

So, I'm being nice, even though I know Sam's not smart, being manipulated like this. My father worked for the government—an egghead engineer, so, of course, his worker *is* stupid in comparison. My father never lost a game of Scrabble in his life, would count cards automatically, multiple numbers in their thousands together in his head. Of course, he made everyone feel not as smart as he was. In fact, he made me feel stupid my entire life.

But now, he can't remember which one is his room. He has lost seven pairs of glasses in two months. Also gone is his dental bridge. He does well when I show him photos from an old green album. He knows every person there, but at Life Care he doesn't recall being married. His wife is there though. Her name is Ruth Ann, but I've only met her for the first time. It confuses him when I tell him Ruth Ann is not my mother-and never has been. She is attended by Sam today too.

"Hey, Sam," I say, "My father used to go on walks every day. Do you think you could take him on a few. I would appreciate it, and I know he certainly would love it. If you could find time, it would be great. I'm going back home tomorrow and won't be back for another few months. How about those Orioles, Sam? They're not doing too well, but they have a good young core...." Sam nods, tells me they're not very good.

I listen to what he has to say, even though I hate baseball. I'm trying very hard for Sam to like me. The Orioles don't stand a chance.

It's a New Year

I'd been forever at home when the *emergency* happened. All I heard was a voice distorting over the cheap Nokia pressed into my head; a voice shouting through the brick. She went to Boston for First Night, again, and I remember one year wrapping three scarves around my head to attend this with her. Hell, maybe it was too cold, maybe the twenty-minute trip from Nahant, too long...but we did other things, other years, than First Night.

Not last year.

I don't know why things happen, and if I did, I'd be some God. I'd be forever at home. I'm no God.

"The icecaps are melting!" I think I hear her say, as if they were disappearing from a giant blow torch.

"Now?" I say. "They are melting now? What can *I* do about that?" It sounds like we are speaking on top of each other. Our voices were once a single harmonious note; now we can't hear one another or be heard ourselves.

"Hello, hello?"

What can I do now? My life is already a flood plain, without assurance, without insurance, without any assistance. I have felt completely alone forever. And how high will the water be? Three feet, four feet, six feet high and rising? She's certainly high enough, and certainly mighty, enough in my mind. Is the water going to get high enough to get to the roof? If I bought into it, will my personal insurance go through the roof?

"Hello? Hello? I can't hear you either. What? Are you drunk?" I say, knowing that there are only two options for her timbre, and one of them is *drunk*.

"The ice-*buzzzzzzzzzzzzzzzz*...Ice-scullllllptures."

"Hello? I still can't hear you. Scriptures? Sculptures?"

Today had been a day. December 31 is always the last day, and meteorologists say it's been warmer than usual everywhere on the planet for the last year. Ice is melting everywhere. I worry how to make things right. Often, I never can. In my backyard, the hockey rink I built is now a tarp and a puddle. With no boundaries, the water has spread and seeped under the rink's plywood boards. I see it all too clearly when I walk outside by the puddle, thinking that all things eventually crumble like the mighty sculptures at the Parthenon. Missing arms, heads, and totally broken legs, almost unrecognizable.

On the phone, you are my Athena with bad reception. Now that I'm outside I can see and hear everything.

"The fucking ice sculptures are melting. This sucks!" she yells, when the reception allows me to hear what she's actually saying. When I ask her to come over, she hangs up, as if I have completely misunderstood everything.

After Getting High

We had lunch at Pizzapalooza, which made us think about how many other spin-offs there were.

So, my friend Trey, who knows a lot of things about a lot of things, happens to know a lot of Paloozas. He mentioned Polar Palooza, then Pet-a-Palooza, and Learn-A-Palooza, the SAT prep course. He certainly didn't forget Puff-a-Palooza, a 24-hour marathon of vintage Sid and Marty Krofft Productions run on Classic Nickelodeon.

"Dude," we say to Trey, "what-the-fuck-are-you-a loser-Palooza?"

Then my date laughed and aspirated. Trey knew the Heimlich, and while she choked, the wind ruffled in the outside trees until a leaf spiraled off, the same time as the pizza was expelled, just like that.

Can Anybody Do Anything?

When something happened to my wife I rushed her to Doc Snickens, the only person I knew who had a Miracle Cure named after him. It was just whiskey. I hadn't seen Snickens in a while, and he hadn't aged well. My beloved wasn't doing well either, and by the time I reached the camp, neither was I, exhausted from carrying her over my shoulder from the road to the camp. Wolfboy knocked Maggie, known as "The Amazing Woman with No Arms or Legs," out of her wheelbarrow and told me to lie my dear sweet Lassaretta down, and he would wheel her the rest of the way to Snickens.

Doc was sitting on the gate of his wagon car, eyes closed, head back, a bottle of whiskey on the ground at his feet.

"Doc! Doc! You gotta help me!" I was shaking him.

Snickens snorted and rolled over, as if still on his hay bed, and fell off the wagon onto the ground next to the bottle. "Is that Lassaretta?" he squinted, remembering it had been years since Lassaretta and I ran off and left the circus. "I don't see her chest rising," he assessed.

"Do something!" I said.

Snickens went and got a new bottle while Wolfboy dumped my wife from the wheelbarrow to the ground. Then he held Lassaretta's mouth open with his hairy hands as Snickens tried to get her to drink. She could neither swallow nor spit it out as the Miracle Cure rose up and overflowed from her like a clogged kitchen drain.

"There's nothing I can..."

"What?" I yelled, as Snickens guzzled whatever was left of the bottle of Miracle Cure.

"It's just whiskey," I heard a faint voice say from the ground. It was only Maggie. Then Wolfboy sheepishly lifted her from the ground into her wheelbarrow, her head and neck scanning and straining over the wooden side rails.

Encasements, Compartments, Boxes

The tissue box lies crushed in the back seat of the Subaru my father used to drive. He stopped when we forced him to, but he was forgetting how to get to places. Now he forgets he even owned that car.

The tissues hang out like innards from an animal crushed on a country road. The cardboard casing has been run over by my guitar case and my overnight bag, as they get the backseat treatment.

At my girlfriend's, we play music at night until it is time to put on my pajamas. I never carried tissues in my car and these seem almost unusable, fanned out of what used to contain them. The sunny yellow box was initially purchased by my mother when she was still alive. My father blows his nose in a handkerchief.

I know people who have lost babies and kept the nursery forever. Or dead children's rooms became museums, retaining posters of the teen idols from *Creem Magazine*. Some wives keep their husband's clothing within plastic to maintain the smell of their departed darlings. Every few days they unzip to sniff.

I chauffeur a tissue box from my father's last car that will stay there until it no longer runs. I'm frozen whenever I see it. I cannot throw it out, nor can I use it up. It stays there, crushed.

The Resigned Life of a Condo Trustee

The Department of Public Works phones me about the army of trash marching in the yard of one of the units. It started as a few pieces of a living room, then it humped into more: a Frigidaire with door attached, then a dining room table with smashed chairs looking victim to an axe murderer. Then some televisions, and finally, a foam-bearing sofa.

I say, "I know a few things. It reminds me of the Bronx in the '70s. It shouldn't, I mean, this is Dedham, but all we need is shirtless children bouncing on the springs of a thread-bare mattress." I know this first hand because I saw a film during that time period, when I studied Sociology in college. It was a time when I was too scared to actually visit the Bronx.

"It is Dedham," she says.

"The owner's from Brookline," I say. "Money."

"He can go dump it other places. They closed the Dedham Transfer a few months ago."

"COVID?"

"No, disrepair," she says.

We can now drive our trash elsewhere...not in *our* neighborhood. "That's how it is now," I say. "We don't need a research study to know that."

She hangs up.

I get another call from The Board of Health. The abandoned dishwasher looks dangerous. It's on the lawn with a knife in it.

"Isn't it just sitting there?" I ask.

"It's dangerous, and if the dishwasher runs outside with a knife, the police will get involved."

I get involved instead. I call the unit owner's voice mail and Mister Whites', the realtor trying to sell all the open units. He can't do anything about the trash. Whites says his people have no interest in living there.

"Oh, it's a fine neighborhood..."

"Until the trash arrived," Whites interrupts.

"I know how it is," I say, "It'll take a lot to do that. We may need to involve the courts, but the courts aren't hearing anything because of the pandemic. Let me see if anything can be done."

I put on a mask and walk around the corner, and see the pile has expanded. An old wedding dress sits in the dirt, and every so often the white chiffon catches the wind, making it a tumble weed. Another new addition is a rusted old Volkswagen, which has an extension cord running from one of the units into a small refrigerator located in the backseat.

"Hey!" I yell to a man in a car.

"Fuck you, it's my right to not wear a mask," he yells back.

"That's not what I was going to say."

"And I'm not quarantining two weeks either. I intend to leave her and go to the store. That's my right too!"

"Okay," I tell him, and walk back home, the filing cabinet, my destination. When I return, I give him a folder. "Here you go, and welcome. The rules and regulations for the association are there, so please follow them. The condo fee is due the first of the month, and it's considered late on the fifteen. In the winter, when it snows..."

The Drowning Girl

Alejandra walks the perimeter of the pond about once a month since *it* happened, more often in the winter, as it is a much more difficult thing for her to do in the summer. It's a 1.5 mile hike, and she estimates she has gone over 200 total miles on these walks. During the first year, she would sit completely opposite to the beach across the pond and speak to the drowning girl, but as the years have gone by, she has brought herself to the beach's edge to talk right close to where she drowned.

She would be in her early twenties today, the drowning girl, as Alejandra remembers exactly how she looked, but not her exact age when *it* happened. The girl appears to her in dreams as a coffin floating in the water, bobbing around at a length up to an adult's knees. How long had she bobbed there? In the dream it seems like forever. Alejandra thinks about that often, but can't come up with an answer. It couldn't have been that long.

After *it* happened, Alejandra tried therapy. She was told to handwrite a letter to the drowning girl. The whole thing felt stupid and impossible. The following week's therapy was an hour away when Alejandra tried to start the assignment; that's what it felt like to her...an *assignment*, not something which had the slightest chance of making anything feel better or making anything go away. Pen in hand, she impeccably wrote "Dear" perfectly at the top left of her journal. Then she put the pen down and looked at the page.

Dear...Dear...Dear...Dear,

She then gave the book a toss and stayed in her room until the hour was up, perfectly missing her appointment and never rescheduling with her therapist again.

When she speaks to the drowning girl, she looks into the water. Sometimes the day is bright, and blue, the water clear, the way it was on that day, yet other days it is not clear at all. Being a lifeguard was her very first job. She loved the red one-piece bathing suit. It felt to her as if she had arrived. The day *it* happened, it was 100 degrees, and the girl she was assigned to work with had called out. Alejandra knew she had been out with Franco, a not very cute lifeguard. He had a bottle of vodka hidden in his truck he had stolen from his parents for their date. The sweat was rolling out from underneath her dark hair, down her back, and the pond was packed with people trying to beat the heat. In fact, it was wall-to-wall people on the sand, and just as many packed in by the shoreline. Alejandra was being very diligent scanning the water, even when some middle-school boys pretended to play some fake game near her tower. She knew the tricks of older boys, like the not very attractive co-worker, but also the tricks of the younger boys, just wanting to be in proximity of her so they could imagine her later that day when they were alone in their bedrooms.

It was in mid scan of the water that Alejandra saw her. She was face down, her tiny sundress appearing like a wet paper towel, and her floppy white hat ebbing slightly against the pond's current. Alejandra felt an urge to yell, as that might be quicker, then the thought was to blow her whistle, but she knew that made no sense, and it was up to her to do what she was trained to do. As she sprung up, to leap down from the tower, she was late getting to the water.

Pushing off the bottom step of the tower, her right foot slipped ever so slightly, sending her sprawling face down into the sand.

It was viewed as not her fault, and the Department of Recreation was investigated for not making sure there were enough lifeguards on that day, but that was it. She wasn't fired, nor did she quit, but she doesn't remember the job ending. Alejandra avoided reading any of the local newspaper accounts, and the girl's name remained pushed away from her memory.

She also couldn't feel love or be loved by anyone. There were the losers or abusers, where, also, she could leave at any time. The need to be in any sort of relationship ended at the point of the drowning girl, and now, at her age, she only had one real commitment, to walk the oval around the pond, and to speak to the drowning girl.

Beautiful Prayers

There is beauty in prayers that are answered, but it's ugly things that have better odds of coming true. There is something exquisite about even a maggot.

There is a spiral staircase going around and around. You never should try to go up or down because you'll get stuck in the middle.

He wants you to stop spinning. Have an escalator or an elevator in your house, but sometimes use the stairs. There are options.

Even if you have money, you pray to win the lottery. You can rob a bank, because you used to work in one and know some tricks. The woman up the street with dark roots was fatally shot trying to rob one.

A butterfly in the sun, over a lake, is a beautiful thing but the moth in your closet wasn't. New clothes don't have holes. You caught the moth in a tiny paper cup. It lived and died in Dixie.

Depression wrote this short paragraph. No one understands it. You crumbled it up and threw it away.

Prayers are not just wishes.

God wants you to know that.

The New Coach

Jimmy Grant answered a job listing for "Sobriety Wellness Coach" he'd seen posted at the hospital where he attended meetings a few times a week. He was sober, and finally well, but as often is the case, he wasn't very employable given his history. The wording of the ad was quite curious and noted, "You will be compensated through a multi-billion dollar organization." This could mean two things. 1) He would be compensated well, or 2) The job was going to be part of a research study for the greater good.

When he was called for a video interview, Jimmy thought they were going a bit over the top with the "coach" part of the job title, as the wall behind Mr. Samuelson was covered with banners and posters of players. Jimmy recognized most of them, being a fan, and he couldn't help but talk to Samuelson about Ryne Sandberg and Ernie Banks, who were posted prominently in the office. *My middle name is Ryne!* Jimmy wanted to yell, but he had to remember that this was still an interview and not to get too excited. Then, damn if their conversation didn't end up heading in the direction of Jerome Walton and Tuffy Rhodes. Jimmy thought this might be bad form, but if it didn't get him the job, at least he'd had a good conversation about baseball, a pastime that always passed the time for him. The only odd part of the interview was when Samuelson asked for his blood type, and was thrilled it was AB-negative. Besides that, it all seemed on the level.

The next day, he was contacted for a second interview, to be held at 1060 West Addison Street, which he immediately knew as the address of Wrigley Field. Jimmy realized that the job was going to be with the Cubs. *It's likely some training position, where once or twice a year, you tell your story so the players will know how much they have to lose.* Jimmy thought. *More likely it is going to be collecting urine samples used for drug tests.*

Even the worst of these possibilities, Jimmy knew, was better than his current sober job as barista at Windy City Coffee. He was pumped. All he had to do is tell Samuelson his story of sobriety, which he'd been told at meetings was very entertaining, and this job would be his. *I have experience, strength, and hope,* Jimmy said as he entered Marquee Gate, as instructed, at the intersection of Addison and Clark.

Samuelson's office was plush, with a soft, royal blue sofa, and the posters on the wall he recognized from the video interview. When Jimmy responded to the question on his experience, and began to tell the complete story of his drinking and drugging, Samuelson cut him off. "Look," he said. "Let's be honest. Your job is going to be working directly with Greg Mustange. Ever hear of him?" he said, and winked.

"Greg Mustange!" Jimmy yelped, then worried he was too loud. "He had 59 homers last year, and is one of my favorite players because he overcame so much, but wait...has he relapsed or does he just need a sponsor?"

"Sobriety Wellness Coach, and you would work directly with Greg and with us. You would travel with the team, make sure Greg does what he's supposed to. We can't have any more photos in strip clubs or ones of snorting coke off supermodels. Best thing about all this, and the job is that it's all sanctioned by Major League Baseball. I mean, they don't want the mess...we don't want the mess. It's bad publicity."

"So, will I be going to meetings with him, perhaps spiritual talks?"

"Well, not exactly," Samuelson said.

"I hope you're not expecting me to police him and knock drinks out of his hands?" Jimmy asked.

"No, not at all."

"Okay, good." Jimmy said, relieved.

"Good," Samuelson echoed. Now, there will just be a few more things we must check on." Samuelson picked up his phone, and turned to Jimmy, "You want this job, right?"

"Of course," Jimmy said.

"We're ready," Samuelson said into the phone.

In less than a minute, a nurse carrying a rubber tourniquet and phlebotomy tray entered. "You may not know this," said Samuelson, "because it's confidential medical information, but since we're working on the same team...Mustange's blood-type is AB-negative."

"Same as mine!"

"...and if we need blood from you, at any time, or urine, at any time, you are the guy. MLB will no longer look at players struggling, or using, or relapsing, or anything. It's bad for the game and the fans don't like it. Mustange is just one of baseball's high profile players. He was heading to be the face of the game and the face of the Cubs. The last thing the league needs is another '80s Pirates or Mets scandal. If the league is clean, everyone is clean and baseball is clean. Every single team will employ a Sobriety Wellness Coach for each blood type too."

Samuelson produced a contract from his satchel. "Just sign here, and initial next to the line that says that you agree to be blood and urine tested every week. Of course, it's a one strike and you're out policy."

Jimmy held the document. He scanned down, noted Greg Mustange's name, and paused. Jimmy had worked hard to change, to be honest, and to live his life in the best way possible. That's what a Twelve Step program is all about. He read the contract in more detail, and it struck him that if he signed and honored the contract, he would be acting honestly, and not doing anything he wasn't supposed to do.

"Do I get to meet Greg Mustange?" Jimmy asked.

"Oh, at least a few times a week."

Jimmy took the pen, and in his neatest handwriting signed his name, "James Ryne Grant."

The Tinkerer

The house Dan Dobler grew up in was right down the street from where he lived now. As a good neighbor, he would do things such as mow the lawn there and shovel the driveway. The neighbor was grateful, but what did she know?

She knew upgrades. She upgraded with new cabinets, a center island, and marble countertops. There was even a library replacing the boyhood bedroom Dobler used to sleep in. Next thing needing to be done was painting the outside shingles. They were peeling, weathered, and $20,000 of work. About 10 grand short, she instead reached for the next fix, a vacation in Europe.

It made sense that Dobler was asked to watch the house while she was away. He did these things even if it felt as if his skin were covered with an itchy rash. He hated that the outside still needed work, and he hated it was green. It had been yellow when his family was there. Dobler went to The Home Depot.

The neighbor came back from her trip,and saw the house was freshly painted. She would have preferred it to stay green, but it had been done at no cost to her, and it looked no longer battered. At $20,000 it could be whatever color she wanted. With the savings she immediately booked another vacation.

The old, removed cabinets were stored in the garage. Dobler told her he needed the area as a central base for the painting. She didn't want the cabinets, but they couldn't be put out on trash night because of being a bulk item. The next night trash was due, she noticed the front driveway was bathed with a bright explosion from a new floodlight.

During the next trip, Dobler re-installed the old, and knocked out the center island in the kitchen. When she returned, she demanded it all be put back. He thought about it, agreed to fix it during the next week when she was back at work. That first day, Dobler moved a twin bed into the library with a few metal models of fighter jets on the shelves—a poster of Carl Yastrzemski hung on the wall.

At the arraignment her attorney used the term "squatting," which wasn't exactly correct and he was ordered to vacate. In a few days, Dobler returned, violating the judge's order, and was walking around the driveway activating the floodlight's motion sensors until the light's beacon mixed in with the ones that were blue and flashing.

The Strength of a Single Lion

A Political Jaunt

The word "lion" is a part of the word "million." It's not pronounced *Mil-lion*. I wish the word meant a million lions instead. A million. You wouldn't stand a chance against even one. At the circus we make lions stand on platforms. It's great that they do this because they want to eat the fuck out of you.

The gold in the ringmaster's uniform tonight is blinding from the lights. If everyone would hold up one gold nugget, what would it be worth?   A million? The ringmaster's announcement is the first thing people heard tonight. He is the star of the circus, the main course, and I, in comparison, am only an appetizer.

Anyway, I'm standing under the haunches of a lion, and I'm thinking, one quick move and I'm diving between his back legs, thinking it is a possible escape route. Lions are only cats, giant cats, but then again, even my house cat, if I have one false move during play, she will scratch the shit out of me. My friend, a Chihuahua owner, used to warn people too, but they would try to pet her dog anyway. It didn't go well.

As I'm thinking all of this, the lion is licking his lips, and his tongue is huge, the size of a bath towel. I'm a little bony nugget, a fillet to him, but he's trained to do what he does. He wants to listen. In fact, I've forced him to. The ringmaster is quiet, while the cat stands. The crowd leans in, amazed, as that is what I'm hired to do: to amaze them. Some of them are, and some are excited that this could go either way. They are like people who enjoy watching NASCAR because they want to see crashes. The ringmaster is the real pro here. He will whisper to the crowd until the lion does a trick, then his voice will rise, encouraging the audience to cheer and to scream their approval.

I've thought this a million times. The crowd is just like the lion, well-trained and choreographed. I'm waiting for it, the next thing I am supposed to hear—the ringmaster's voice exploding over the P.A. system. Instead I hear feedback and feel pain in my head. It's not from the sound. It's the cat. He has delivered a rebuttal with his giant paw. I see a small piece of my scalp spiraling from my head. My brain is already gone. I hear the last thing I will ever hear. It is the crowd roaring.

Airport 20/20

It's that part on television or in the movies when a decision is made. The character says, "I'll be at Gate 12," or, "It's flight 421," and the love interest, or potential interest, will either show up or not be there.

That's the drama.

The cliffhanger.

This trip was a different story. It was planned with each other, and you were to meet at the gate, which was the perfect opportunity for her not to show.

The trip was planned on Christmas, and 2020 happened because neither of you could stop it. Right after commitment to the trip you made love to each other, or rather had sex, against the wall, she telling you after that if someone else came along it would be okay with her if you went for it. You quickly processed that as bad, and from now on you'll have to walk on eggs—but not eggshells, as the saying goes, because eggshells were already broken, and it's a stupid phrase anyway, but you said, "No it wouldn't be, okay."

Alone at security, you were held, because you were nervous and sweaty. They patted your socks, pulled down your pants, as other passengers walked by, seeing you in your underwear between the hinges of the temporary partition, as another thirty-three minutes passed. Boarding time was announced, and you ran to Gate 12, stopping, hands on knees, panting as you saw her, standing to the right of where you embark, a perfect vision, staring at you, hardly breathing.

Annual Cookout

(Sung to a nursery rhythm)

Madeline brings elephant wings, the recipe she stole from her mother. The dish to be funny, but Madeline's not cunning, and her act just makes me feel dumber. Perhaps its word flicking, the food's really chicken, and the bad joke is getting my goat. She presents the food gaily, pretending it not fairly, obvious gray matter she's serving.

I brought some mayonnaise to simply amaze, the folks who brought spuds needing somethin'. I hope for muffins which I want to be stuffing into my mouth so early this morn.

What to do when the guests are few, though later there's bunches for luncheon. Madeline's drunk already and asks about Betty, knowing full well of the hell of our parting. Remember that time she swallowed a lime when we did those shots of tequila? But never real love just an urge and a shove of Madeline's grabbing a wiener. Betty went nutty but *we were just buddies*, just coddling down with a bottle. I never will trust, Betty lectured to us, then flipping me down like a dealer.

When this party began, I ate Madeline's thangs, tasting better than I ever remember. I waved off coleslaw, saying I had some before, as Madeline laughed like a weasel. We'll see about that—going tit for a tat, Madeline's pride just wanting revival. You hide, I'll seek, she stood by the sink while conducting my business I stood for. Haste and not waste when she grabbed the toothpaste, my lips getting sucked through a mint phase. My mind flashed to Betty, I felt guilty again, it was five years ago she'd discovered— Madeline uncovered after serving her mother's elephant wings on that day in the summer.

The First Four Steps Walking up a Cliff

If you ever dreamed of committing suicide copy all people, like a mimeograph. Smelling the chemicals off the paper in first grade, was my first high, but now people I've harmed spin around and around like the drum of that blue-inked machine. Who? Now? Later? Never? They are all carbon copies anyway. I'll copy all the people I've affected with my behavior.

Copy all, and add people. Add things. Add each resentment I've had in my life. Add all my bad conduct. That about covers everything I've ever harmed. Write it, only once, and multiply it times one, because anything times one is itself. That's known as identity property.

How do I know I'm ready, when I'm not ready? For one thing, I'm not ready to catch this virus. It's 2020 and the spring will turn to summer, then turn to fall, and it's like the world is in a blackout. Time passes, but I won't know where it went. I know where I am right now. Today I waited six feet from others to buy Raisin Rosemary Crisps at Trader Joe's, which I'll later spread with orange pub cheese. It's the closest I'll get to a pub these days. The cheese is soft, like I am. Soft, like the sand on the beaches I grew up near.

Today, I go to the store—and I can buy the cheese. I remember having to steal food when I was out of money. I used my cash on other things. Buying food was a luxury. My check book was referred to as my book of free coupons as I had a zero balance. It felt like walking within range of a hidden camera, while knowing, during that time, you were visible. Those were some unseen steps which I took right there.

I know I've never been ready. I didn't pray. I used to pray for things, but it was like asking for gifts at Christmas from Santa Claus. I'd stayed up all night, to listen for the noise on the roof, a sleigh landing, heavy boots on the shingles. There's an awful empty feeling, in the morning, of not hearing anything.

It's this emptiness that led me to doing the things about it I'll later regret, noted in the work as my bad conduct. I cheated, and lied. I was selfish. It's all on the list I am writing. I guess there's the sex conduct list to write about next, but I don't want to write about the fucking... the...fucking...sex...conduct. I swear, some of it is too appalling, especially when seen in a notebook. I swear. Fuck. Was it a joke back then? Two drunks enter a bedroom, but only one of them was drunk. The room spins.

Today I don't know if I can keep doing this, dear people, whom I've cc'd, and bcc'd. I'm barefoot, walking up stone stairs to the very top. The cliff is high, and there's a small inlet where the water rushes in. I'm scared. There's no one there to catch me if I jump. When the moment is right, I may. I'll have to time it, or if I'm gambling, I'll hurl off the rock at any random time. I will sail in the air, feeling the speed, and the coldness, while falling. I am hardly invincible. I know I will count the time free falling.... One one-thousand...Two-one-thousand...Three-one-thousand... Four-one-thousand...One one-thousand again, if it goes too long...and hope the water fills up beneath me, so when I hit, it's there to catch me and slap me in the face.

Kill the Baby Makers

The idea was half-baked, semi-fossilized, yet somehow there was a timekeeper lodged in her head. She realized it, but knew it wasn't her just being crazy. *Crap,* she thought. *Is this what they mean about the biological clock? Am I at that point in my life?*

Being all about appearances, she thought, she needed to re-marry. Her marriage to Steve had not ended because he didn't want children; it was because she had killed him. On the flip side, she didn't kill him because he didn't want children.

His death looked like an accident, his twisted body lying at the foot of the basement stairs, all askew. She pushed him down thirteen steps, leaving his body somehow looking like a swastika. Even though he deserved it, her first thought was to find a lawyer, a good intermediary, but as it turned out, she would never need one, as she was wearing an apron when the police arrived. All kinds of Betty Crocker shit going down.

The clock was ticking. Better to push her body to reproduce than to be sitting alone in jail. *Tic-toc.* Time moving slowly when locked up—but then, she thought, *What happens if I hate my new baby maker? What if he is abusive?* Steve had been that way, and that led him to his launch down the cellar stairs. *Well, now I can have a baby,* she thought, and *the rest will take care of itself.*

On a dating website she left-swiped everyone named Steve and any men who didn't want children. When she came across a Steve who also didn't want children, she threw her phone down in disgust and thought she might have broken it. When she picked it up, the phone had refreshed the web browser, and because of her recent

Internet history, it opened to a page of cookie recipes. A blinking ad for a new app called *BabyMaker* also caught her eye. She thought, *karma,* signed up, and was welcomed to the site "*where babies are made from babes.*"

On *BabyMaker*, there were plenty of prospects who listed relationship preferences as short-term, long-term, or "no-terms-whatsoever." *Too bad there is no long-term, with the possibility of short-term*, she laughed, as she took a swipe to the left on a dude, without a shirt, standing by a Lexus.

By the time she had closed the app, an hour later, she'd had it with men. Maybe a no-terms-whatsoever type of relationship would work best. Maybe. She went to check her e-mail and found 108 from the *BabyMaker* site plus two spam messages. The first piece of spam had a link about a group for women who felt perfectly happy with having no children, and the second one was for increasing the sperm count of your partner to boost your chances of pregnancy. *Partner?* she scoffed.

Then she started on the now 119 e-mails from "perspectives," and was bombarded with crude messages and anatomy. She wondered if she should invite any of them over to push them down the stairs. Disgusted, she lingered over the women happy without children link. *Childless by Choice* did not cost anything, and at no risk to her or anyone else, she waved the arrow over the link, and over, and over, again, until her battery ran out.

The Pillows of Society

I told my daughter that if I get to be as bad as my father to take a pillow and suffocate me. I told my son too. I will tell anyone who will listen because I don't want to lose the ability to think, to remember—to have dignity as much as he has.

Now I'm worried. I'm forgetting things. Today I had to google nearly every pop culture reference which used to fly from my brain and out of my mouth. No one has asked me for my car keys. Yet.

In the world of "yet," we are all being assessed as we grow older. Things that have not happened yet, but they will. Some people don't own pets because animal's life expectancy is less and too heartbreaking to live through. Yet, we do, and we wait, and it happens. Some people trust the health care system and die like animals.

I started to leave myself notes on the refrigerator— when bills are due and such. One says "buy more refrigerator magnets." There is another reminding the kids to buy or wash all the pillows. I hope when they are prepared, it'll be a day I'll have no idea why I wrote it.

Times Square During Lunch Hour

A man on the street cries out through a dirty, crusted face about the war going on each day within his mind. He sits hidden by a canopy of darkness where no one will enter, even to offer up money he wouldn't see...because he's busy: a one man play in many acts, much more real than a show on Broadway or any church sermon. Forget the damnation because he's living it, preaching with vinegar and spit, which narrowly misses him, from the mouth of the businessman with a cold.

I am as close as anyone will get to him for the next hour, as if there is a pane of glass between him and them and that glass needs cleaning. Remember when Giuliani removed the windshield cleaning bums from the streets for a better New York? Hell, we won't miss them, but they might miss us. On this October day it all seems odd the sun being as bright as it is against the filthy green of his jacket. Today, we are blind through our squint, and I only hear him speaking loudly about important things, his sons and daughter, a wife and a dog he once had in the house on Long Island in a town I once lived in.

"And, fuck you, man, you don't know the least of it," he says, "that's right, that's right, these streets are lonely and there once was a woman I loved like the moon." He staggers. "...and the stars. If I had a rocket I would fly there right now, to find her once more, right now!"

No one is listening.

"As the only good women you find are up there...on the moon, but, fuck her...she was too damn political. And you know, when Nixon was still President the world was as flat as bread—yet dynamic like the round top of a freshly baked..."

He stops, hesitates as if the transmission of his car has skipped. "One time I met the president," he says. "I shook his hand on a missile line in Dayton, Ohio. Nixon said, 'you are helping save the world,' but we obviously didn't do shit, and his hand wasn't as sweaty as you might imagine but we all knew how slimy he would become. When that dog died, which was the beginning of the end for me, I wish I had gone with him—in a paper box I found further west near the bend of a river, down in the wet, muddy ground, which ran a long ways. I wish I could lie there now, so I can focus on the stars. Always focus on the stars, they only shine for your wishes."

Later, he said he drove a Ford Escort across the country with the dog that he loved dying in the back seat. "I drove away from them, and I didn't look back....Now I look back all the time, as you never know what might be gaining on you...Satchel Paige said that."

I folded my lunch bag as the man continued, his voice fading in the distance, "Now he was a guy whose life came at you at different angles, a master of deception pitching in the "Negro League," with some great ballplayers. None of them got to the bigs till past their prime..."

I was late getting back to work, listening to this man. He told stories the way that a modern day Will Rogers might, and only I got that—from stopping.

Predators and Prey

There she is, sitting there like a stuffed owl. "They only act like they're stuffed," she says, "not moving, big eyes..."

"Ever see one of them in action?" I ask.

She moves to her phone and brings up a video, *Owl Attacks Fearless Rabbit.*

"That's more about the rabbit," I say.

"No, look," she says. "It says the owl's talons can have a pressure force of about 500 pounds per square inch."

As the owl descends the rabbit leaps over the diving predator at the point of attack. *Perhaps its family is nearby or maybe the rabbit is just a tough guy, who loves a good fight,* the video says.

When the video stops she says, "They don't show the end."

Perfect Crimes from an Imperfect Man

When Hal was about fifteen, he'd heard the best place he could set a fire was at the factory that made trick birthday candles, the ones that would ignite after you blew them out. Certainly there would be overtime for security on re-flash watch, and extra observation time for Hal to enjoy in the crowd.

At 25, he heard the best day to rob a bank was Halloween. When he decided to hit the Eastern Bank on that day in 2005, no one questioned his wearing two masks. No one was at all suspicious of him, except the head teller he passed the note to. On the rear camera it looked like he had pulled his rubber mask down, which he did, and no one except employees on the teller line and the front camera could see he wore a mask under the one he had pulled down. The newspapers described him as having "multiple personalities."

In a crowd, during loud fireworks was the best time to shoot someone in the back, so Hal shot his girlfriend's lover on the Esplanade on the 4th of July. It was in front of the guy's family and a million random people. By the time anyone noticed, Hal was moving like a pinball, running through the crowd with no one knowing the reason.

And it was perfect watching the news of it on television while sitting with his girlfriend. It was minutes before she could speak, but he tried to engage her in conversation about the hotdog eating contest, whether the buns really counted. "Perhaps if they were toasted," he said to her and smiled when she said nothing.

Ambien Beatle

I am the egg man
They are the egg men
I am the walrus
Goo goo g'joob

She just said that she sprang up out of sleep, and finished a thought out loud to me, but I'm between white, cool, and clean sheets. I went into a dream. Currently, I'm not there. Her thought was, *you're going to get it when I get home.*

"So, what did you just say? I don't remember," I ask her. The seat is cool against me, and there are flashing lights through the kaleidoscope. My sleeping pills give me that—all kinds of illusions. Living is easy with eyes closed.

"No, what did *you* just say? I took a few Ambien. I know what it's like to be dead," she responds.

"What is when I get home?" I am asking. There are a few windows to the side of me, and there are raindrops crying, sobbing silently. They slither while they pass.

"You're going to get it." I remember that was something she said, but was it a come-on or a warning. We seem to be with each other simultaneously even when we aren't. We are all together, but nothing's going to change the world. I am here, and you are here...*wait that's not right!*

Are you here? You are in a bed, by a window, with flannel sheets, window open to the night sky. The moon has blue lights. You reach out and hold my hand; it's warm. The vinyl seats are cold against my boxer shorts. Last thing I remember, I'm slipping between my bed sheets like a piece of lettuce between refrigerated bread.

Now, I'm swimming like a corn flake.

We drove—I remember picking you up. I remember climbing out of bed, suddenly. Yesterday...came suddenly. And I saw her standing there right before getting into my car. Now, I see her getting escorted out. Mr. City Policeman, sitting, pretty little policemen all in a row. There is no train, but there definitely is a station. This is definitely a station.

The Cost of Love

When he committed himself, after his breakdown, he had left the rental car parked on some street in Los Angeles. When he signed himself out, to go home, he thought he lost his car for good. It was a solid rental car he'd driven for three years. He called police and towing companies, but he was told the car was someplace in Los Angeles. Someplace, he had no idea.

His next call was to Alamo so he could ask if there was a hidden GPS chip in the car so it could be traced.

"If you rented a car in San Diego or El Paso you might get one," he was told, "but it won't record the information in real time because that encourages unwanted stalking behavior. The chip can tell where the car has been only, so if you turn it in, they will know whether you'd been to Mexico or not. Then you will have to pay for "Loss of Use." That's all they care about. Sometimes we plant a chip in the borrower."

He went back to Alamo to rent another car so he could drive around and locate the previous one, explaining he had loved that car very much, but he felt kicked to the curb. He could no longer drive it in the bliss and love he once had.

"Wasn't it you that had left it high and dry? Your mental illness certainly caused lapses in good judgment," the young woman at the counter added. "You had a chip."

"Well, can you drive me around to save me a new car. I've narrowed it down a little bit," he said. "I'm hoping to find that old love once more."

"It's a loss. You are going to pay for it forever," was the woman's final answer.

How to Stop Birds from Flying into Windows

The bird flew into the window, and Jason thought it was a rock being tossed.

Jason thought a rock was tossed because of what was on the news.

What was on the news couldn't be hushed.

A police officer had shot a black man during a traffic stop.

The man was reaching for something in the back of his car.

The pink lettered frosting, "Congratulations Glenn," was smeared.

A cake had slid when he was stopped for turning on NO TURN ON RED.

No time to rearrange the stuff in the car. He was late and there wasn't time.

The man really liked the person he had bought the cake for.

The words "Congratulations Glenn," were smeared.

The cake was placed in the back seat of the car because the front seat was untidy.

There was a party to honor someone's first year of sobriety.

The police in this town would drink Friday nights, all except Glenn.

Jason's partner had stopped going out with the squad.

Jason's partner's DUI was kept quiet.

A teenager was killed by a drunk driver.

A year ago it was a hit and run.

Glenn left the bar because he hated conversing.

The offender had been at the bar for hours.

Someone at the bar had sat next to Glenn and spoken of screens.

Screens eliminate reflections on office building windows.

Billions of birds die annually from flying into windows.

Hey, Benni

Benni and Nora were in bed, he knowing she was annoyed. Annoyed is a whitewashing understatement. The television colored the dark room.

"The Smarts still hold hands," she said. "I saw them walking hand-in-hand near the apple orchard."

"Good for the Smarts," Benni said. He reached out for her hand, but she pulled it away. "Some people will always do a public display of affection, and *display* is a key word here. Not to bury the lead, but you don't have to google to know of Cortana's affair...with her personal assistant, no less. She even named her son after him."

"Well I don't remember the last time *we* held hands," Nora said, ignoring the entire siring thread.

"It was at the movies. No, wait, it was at Bixby's funeral...no, it was...."

"See?"

Benni didn't want to take this down Memory Lane. He remembered the last time they had sex. It was a long time ago, so how could he forget?

"You know the two are related," Nora added as if she were reading his mind.

"I'll hold your hand if you want," he said.

"No," she replied.

Benni leaned back and watched her face strobe blue, or green, or whatever color was flashing in the show they were streaming. They never seemed to be able to share shows anymore either, both falling asleep at different times, then neither of them able to find the spot without a placeholder.

"If a streaming service would save the point you dozed off, I'd use that service," Benni said. "...or even lost interest."

"That's a can of worms which I hope never gets opened. Too much monitoring of us as it is," was Nora's response. "I'd only want you to, if you wanted to," she repeated. She flipped off the television. Benni was asleep.

I Saw Hell

It was on the face of a man pushing a baby carriage and missing the thrills of his previous life. He was in total misery. His name was Yet. I knew him. I said to myself, *Don't ever forget, Yet...yet, don't ever forget.*

I drove, sort of. My car was slow in traffic, and Yet was moving faster than it. I would get ahead, but then end up on the bumper of the car in front of me, and Yet would get halfway up the block, up ahead in the distance. I could have yelled out the window, but during the pauses in driving I sent him a text instead.

"I saw you today," it read, "and I'm just remembering the times we used to have together. You're not missing anything. It was a shit show. Remember when you threw yourself out the window? It was only from the first floor, the fall no more than the flight of stairs leading up to the front doorway. But, hell, you did throw yourself out a window, I mean, who am I to judge that versus someone throwing themselves hundreds of feet. from the top of a bridge."

Need Help Call The Samaritans

One time I called the Samaritans. They told me I didn't need to say anything or do anything. I didn't even have to tell them what was going on, but it might be a good release. I told them, okay, I'm on the phone now and I'm not really good about talking on the phone, nor do I like talking on the phone very much. Their voice was kind and soft at this epiphany. I was grateful when the call ended. I was more uncomfortable than desperate, as it turned out.

I turned left onto another street, and Yet continued down it. In an hour he texted me back. "What the hell are you talking about?" it said.

The Off-Season

There is absolutely no reason to go to a bar during your lunch break except for the obvious twenty. Still, two beers in, I had a tough time looking at the guy down the end wearing a white shirt, green vest, black fedora, and giant, golden bow tie. His pants were bloomers, with a little buckled belt pulled tight around the bottom of each one like a zip tie. His face was bleached out, and his gigantic, silk, gold, bow tie drooped down to his chest.

I shouted, "Hey, aren't you Lucky? The Celtics mascot?"

Lucky looked at me, looked at his beer, back to me, and then back at the beer. It was a non-verbal response, *Yes, asshole, don't you see the season's over, it's mid-afternoon, and I'm not at The Gahhhh-den, I'm in a bar!*

"Weren't the Celtics eliminated last night?" I asked.

"Yes, Captain Obvious," he said.

Lucky, the mascot, was less the costumed prankster, but more of a time-out entertainer for all the fans who couldn't sit a few minutes with their own thoughts during a timeout. All attention would be on him, with his high flying Jet Blue Flight Crew main act. Lucky would run, bounce off a trampoline, soar into the air at twice the height of the basket, do a few flips on the way down and then slam the ball through the hoop. The crowd loved it, but I was much less excited. I always thought he was cheating using that trampoline to upstage the best players in the league. It just wasn't honest.

"So what are you going to do now?" I asked him.

The foam rested on his lip for a full minute, the long delay I knew well, when the reflexes are lost and the brain to tongue connection just didn't work anymore. Then he lapped it off.

"You know, the last Lucky was fired after a drug bust, which was how he made his money in the off-season. I, on the other hand, had an offer at some rodeo in Montana," he paused, "so I must be doing pretty darn good," he said, but I wasn't sure if his smile was sardonic or not.

"Oh, you're much better than that last guy!" my words sprang out of my mouth, as if they were going to cheer him up with a sudden bounce of enthusiasm.

"Well, the rodeo may not work. They don't want me as Lucky, they want me as a clown...*a clown*! They still want me to use the trampoline, but they want me to jump over twenty bulls instead of dunking a ball. I bet they're hoping I'll enhance the show by landing on a bull's horn or something. Shit, I just can't."

"Yeah, why would you do that?" I asked, thinking I'd thrown him a pass for an easy lay-up.

"Because the Celtics own the trampoline!" he said, sounding defeated.

"Well, can you go home and take the summer off? Where do your folks live?

"Centralia...you know, the town that's had an underground fire for over fifty years. I can't go there, but they will never leave."

"Because of the smoldering beneath the surface?

Lucky just looked up at me, as if I were a child making a stupid statement. "Not that. The town was moved to another location, but my parents were one of the seven who refused to move. It went to court. The government will take their home only after they die."

Then we sat as if there was nothing we could do about anything. Then some yahoos came in after work, and they all patted Lucky on the back, and spoke to him with empathy about the lost season. During the break in the action, I remembered it was my son Larry's birthday party this weekend, and my son might really appreciate Lucky in the house. So I asked. "And after, you can hang out with the adults," I added.

"Wow, I really appreciate that. I'd love to have the chance to just be myself. Have a few drinks, hang with you and your family." Lucky paused, but looked sad. "You know during the off season no one knows who I am. The kids think I'm the leprechaun on the cereal box. You know, magically delicious."

"Yeah, I get it. Gotta stay true to who you are, but the good news is you'll not be left out on a lurch. We have one of those round trampolines in the backyard. The springs are a little rusty, and we don't have a hoop, but there's a badminton net..."

Lucky didn't answer, but I forgave him. I only wanted him to have a good off-season.

How You Met Your Husband

You believe in faith, and that everything happens for a reason, so that guy at the end of the bar you've never met before—he is there because you are going to marry him. His clothes are working-man-rugged, but he is not. The thing you do is ignore him. It's messed up, but it's instinctual. You don't want to walk over there, nor do you want him to come to you. That would ruin everything.

His friends have arrived and are throwing money at you—flirting. You know after years working as a bartender, tipping is a lazy way to flirt. Customers are like animals involved in some weird mating ritual, but instead of doing territorial things, or a scent release, even charging you, smashing their skulls into yours, they throw bills on the ground, at your feet, after they've paid you fifteen dollars for their drinks. More of that where that came from baby, when do you get off?

The guy at the end of the bar does not do that. He has ordered, after 45 minutes of you ignoring him, a Budweiser. A simple and stupid Budweiser. Then he motions with his hand for you to move because you're blocking the view of the Rangers-Red Wing game, and it burns you. In fact, your last boyfriend noticed that before you said anything in anger, your face would turn red, but your ears would be redder. He said you were like the steam whistle in Bugs Bunny cartoons when they blow, the metal screaming, twisted and red. It is only after five or ten minutes the color returns like bare branches after fall foliage.

Well, speaking of assholes, you don't reach down, or dare bend over to pick up the tens and twenties off the spongy rubber mat, which smells more like rancid fruit the closer you get to your money. It's intentional so they can catch a good view of your black-panted server butt, or even worse, their way to humiliation: You are prey or predator, dominated or aggressed upon. It is pure hell in the animal world.

That is why you are acting that way for him. You were walking onto your shift, saw him, and begged your friend to stay. "I can't be serving him!" you shout, as your friend looks at you like you were crazy.

"Look," Linda said. "I'm meeting a current boyfriend, so I'm not taking a double shift so you can...I don't know, Bev, so you can do, whatever you think you are doing. Fick that, I'm leaving." How to change curse words is another thing you had to change for this job. Everything is recorded.

"Hey, I was the one who got you this job," you say. "You owe me!" It all makes sense, and it's not just a Hail Mary pass. She should work a double because you know how it is going to play out. All the pieces are in place, but she has decided to not play along, leaving you there to work your shift, and to ignore your future husband. You know it seems crazy, but to you, you've never known anything stronger than the feeling you are having right now.

So, you work the shift. Capture or be preyed upon, prayer answered or not answered. God, the bar is busy now, peeking like the top of a bell curve. On the way down, his friends will leave drunk with empty wallets. You always thought that customers should just dump their wallets out on their way in, but it seems, everyone there is playing it the other way, like a long painful yearning. Like those autumn leaves resting on a lawn that are blown away, the crowd thins out, and it is last call. The target has had only one Budweiser all night. His hockey game ended three hours ago, and it's quiet. All you can hear is your chest thumping, in your ear canal, his ice-blue eyes the engine powering it, the hairs on his arms, with his thick wave of hair are its battery. If he's waiting. But you're not bringing the bill, knowing your behavior is bad enough for termination by complaint. You think you are standing, looking in his direction, but distance seems to be pulling and refracting between the two of you, as you feel you are standing cemented to the ground, when in fact you are walking toward him.

"I've waited," you tell him, seeing his work shirt expanding and deflate, taking in the Universe, then letting it out, "I've been waiting as well," he says. You lean toward him to reply. Your face is less than two feet away.

Up and Atom

On my daily coffee run, I ran into him outside the Starbucks. I'd seen him around the square for 6-8 months, a short homeless guy, Hispanic-mustached. He looked to be young, maybe in his twenties. Today he wore blue sweatpants under denim shorts, the pants too long, and they wrapped around his feet like clouds. He was also harassing everyone near him. "I'm Atom Ant," he yelled, arms pumped over his head. "Atom Ant! Remember him! I'm Atom Ant!" He had a warm, powerful, dark stain on his shirt. The police were on their way.

The next day, on my run, he sat on the thin brick ledge outside the store's large window, near the edge of the sidewalk. "I'm going to start an ant farm," he said, barely audible.

Iconic Folks Talking by a Fire

Elvis, Prince, and Betty White sat by a dying fire, at a camp site. Elvis was pressing a S'mores together, the lava-hot marshmallow ejaculating onto the chubby skin near his palm. Between them, they had had more than everything they could shake a stick at.

"Hey, little man," he said to Prince, "does it bother you that your legacy is found in that Dr. Pepper commercial, with that weird dude in the purple scarf? Isn't he supposed to be you?"

"Paulie Shore," Prince whispered. "Supposed to be him." His face curled into a mischievous, disrespectful curl.

Elvis popped another marshmallow, this one on fire, into his mouth. "Mmmm," he sighed.

"We're icons," Prince added, "but we more represent every man."

"That's a big order, but you're sort of the size of Lisa Marie, when she was born. How's that for iconic."

"You died taking a crap," Betty White snapped at The King. "Don't let him bother you, honey," she said to Prince, who nodded. "We have bigger fish to fry."

"Flart addack, not thit," Elvis said, through his treat. "How blout you?"

"Sometimes men have an urge and they think they have to crap all over the place," Betty said, "but it's really their hearts. They confuse a weak heart with being a shit."

"No, Betty," Prince said. She leaned in so she could hear his quiet voice. "How did you die? You were still okay when I was prowling around."

"Oh, I'm not dead," Betty said. Her voice almost sounded like a chirp. "I may just live forever, doing what needs to be done. We can't just drink *Doc Snickens Miracle Cure* for something as big as this."

The fire shot up and raged suddenly. Some of Elvis's jacket fringe sparked at the ends, ready to go up. "But you're dead."

"You men always thought you'd be in heaven," Betty said. "but, do you know why you're here instead?"

They looked at each other, then looked down. Prince took the red hot poker and stabbed himself, slowly inserting the rod at the speed of a sword devoured by a swallower. Elvis dangled the sleeve of his jacket over the flame and soon he was engulfed. "I'm sorry for everything, Priscilla," he wailed.

Betty gathered up the graham crackers, the Hersey bars, and the marshmallows and placed them in the shopping bag she'd brought from home. "Times have changed, don't you know?" she said. Elvis and Prince returned to the campfire as big men shrinking to normal, only to die again, and again.

Working on a Marriage

When she drove a brush through her hair, she tore out some. She felt she was dying inside, so her husband told her to hold on. He pulled out some of his own, so he would feel what she felt and carried the brush around to keep her right there. "Can you see how that's not helping our marriage?" she said.

"I'm trying," he replied.

Five years ago, during their reception she had popped a Xanax for each one of the wedding dances with each one of her three step-fathers and then passed out. Just thinking of them all needing to be danced with resembled a reception line at a wake, with everyone expressing their condolences.

She knew it would never work. There weren't enough slow songs she liked, so she picked themed music. The rich step-dad, who had left after five years, got "*Take the Money and Run*" by Steve Miller. For the one that raised her more time than the others, "*Seein' My Father in Me*" by Paul Overstreet was felt to be proper. For the dad who hit her mother, Cheap Trick's, "*The House Is Rockin' (With Domestic Problems)*" would be lovely.

The song which the bride and groom danced to, the Lionel Richie, Diana Ross duet, was saved for tonight's anniversary, but like the marriage itself, the record had some skips in it.

To cheer up, they stopped pulling their hair and ate a piece of their frozen wedding cake preserved in the freezer. It was sparkly, white, and the same height as the doorway of the Frigidaire. When she pushed the knife into it, it was impossibly hard, but the knife made a clean cut with no crumbs cascading afterward. They laughed and fed themselves because there was no need for any of the other garbage, after five years—like shoving it into each other's faces. He had ordered flowers, but there was no hairdresser, so she snatched the brush away from him, and kept doing what she had been doing.

Why I am Not a Penguin

When I was cast off by my lover, I asked, "Can we try again?"

"Try living in the Arctic," she said, just like that, "or try staying in the house."

I'm a man that owns penguins. They live in the house. Stuffed animals, plastic toys, and even penguins on my neck tie. None eat squid fish, or krill, or, hell, a pizza? I'm fat enough that women leave me—or are they waiting for me to sit on an egg?

Eggs break, when it's cold out, and it reminds me of something I saw in a documentary. Penguins know to walk with partners for life, in front of a burning sky.

Her Hotel

She bought a hotel, on the ocean, because God told her to. For this, she needed help, so she turned to God, and gofundme.com to raise ten million dollars for the purchase. She decorated her hotel with stars and starfish, or anything having to do with mariners, and the ocean, but mostly stars and starfish. She thought, *God is the stars.*

Her hair was thick and curly and hung down mid-back. He loved to wash it when they shared a tub. After he gently massaged in shampoo, he slowly poured water over her. They both shared this feeling of cleansing. Afterward, they would lay in bed in crisp sheets, the walls as glossed as a blinding light, looked at her ceiling, a flat blue-black, with specs of light painted on it. He drove to her during the first three days of every month, as long as it wasn't the weekend, as the hotel filled during those times. He said he was there because he loved the ocean, but didn't worship it like a God, and he also let it slip that he loved her too.

Before the next month, she told him not to come. It was sudden, He represented too much of her old world, and her spirituality demanded something which she could only describe to him, to make him understand, as something like their bath for seven days a week, twenty-four hours a day, He tried a few times to get in touch with her, even calling the hotel's office, but the recording only said that she/they were no longer taking phone calls, but leave a message if you felt called to do so, and it would be returned if she/they were able and felt called to do so as well.

This all happened because there were things she had never told him. It was a long story, which she had worked through, but it was important for her to be viewed as she was now, never as she was then. Before she was brought to the place she is in now, she used to work as a dental hygienist. She hated the early patients, first thing in the morning. They just rolled out of bed and did nothing to their mouths because they were getting brushed and flossed that day. She hated the patients seen after lunch who only brushed twice a day, and not after lunch. They were the ones that left fish between their teeth. She had no respect for those who didn't have self-care. Mostly it all came down to not brushing and flossing because if everyone brushed and flossed, she wouldn't be needed as much.

The dentist who owned the practice became her lover. He was older, but not yet of the age where he smelled of being old. She liked how he ran the office, paying attention to her and all the employees. He had empathy, even commiserating about the morning and, after lunch, people she despised. The sex was great after hours, on a dentist chair, experimenting with the external oral suction machine, which she was responsible for the sanitizing of afterward. Then the sex was good at his house, and after she moved in the sex wasn't as good. It became his way, and at his times. She also was stunned to realize he wasn't at all the way he was in the office. He was unsupportive, critical, jealous of some of the patients she worked on, and verbally demanding and abusive. She no longer could stand him, but he was her employer, he was her home, and he had become her only lifeline, and he knew it. She felt an urge to do something bad enough to him to land herself in jail, or if she didn't, land herself in an inpatient facility.

The only way possible to leave him was mentally. As long as he thought she was coming on to patients, she thought, why not graze her breasts against the back of the head of a men as she scaled his teeth? Why not whisper in their ears if they seemed responsive to that, about a place to meet later and a time? Why not give herself some sort of control? At first it seemed exciting, almost righteous, but often it brought her to another dark place where she wanted to take the sharp scaling tool and plunge it straight down through the next patient's submandibular duct.

And then came the day, she and her dentist drove up the coast, and something was said, which she can't remember, because he pushed her head hard against the passenger side window causing a concussion. She was in a hospital, and he was nowhere to be seen. When he did come back for her, the next day, she was gone, referred to a woman's shelter on the ocean, run by a group of nuns known to be part of the Maryknoll Sisters. She loved the nuns because of their presence of love and that they gave her space to heal, and meditate, and work her way out of her PTSD. She walked the beach, picking up shells, driftwood and dried starfish. The wood, once important, had ended up, here, exactly where she was, getting grounded in space. This was important, as the sand, the sea, and the stars, gave her peace.

She also began writing a book about overcoming her abuse and broadcasting some of her story on the internet. The segments were heavy and touched on how she had been saved, and her rediscovered faith. She confessed she wanted to be a nun, a key revelation which would become the conclusion of her memoir. People followed her broadcasts, thousands of them, engrossed by her and her story. The nuns also tuned in.

They liked her, but she wasn't Catholic, and that was a good enough reason that she couldn't become one of them. She would do the next best thing. She bought the hotel next door.

The hotel either had guests who loved the ocean, or guests who went there as an instrument of God's teaching, based on her promotion. It was all fine with her, because she believed God was the stars, so why not be the sea, or a man with a beard.

Occasionally she missed the man who had begun to visit, and wanted to have time with him, but then the thought made her feel uncomfortable and confused. She thought maybe it was fear, or perhaps love, but the one with the small "l", not the big "L", which she lived for. She knew, without knowing her story, he couldn't know her, and he could never be the One who knew the number of hairs on her head. She gave her story out to the world, but not to him, which represented something. The day she told him not to come back she already knew, he could never be He.

Beloved Do Us Part

The day my father crashed through the windshield was the day that changed everything. That happened when I was driving him to his funeral. Life is confusing enough without dissecting that statement.

It was windy springtime when the porcelain struck the pavement, shattering, the ashes blowing across Route 3, ending up in the cattails. If some stayed on the highway I couldn't tell where the ashes began and the litter soaking up the oil ended.

She was late going to the church. She hadn't noticed passing me, or my car engulfed in a parade of constrained traffic, which felt more like the participants waiting at the starting point for the parade to begin. Either way, she hadn't noticed the scene. She hadn't paid attention to me much when I was preoccupied recently either. She was attending only because of my father. We were both pretty sick in different ways she said, the day I told her he had left his body.

I was a bit banged up, but I wasn't as bad as Dad. He suffered. Even after death the entirety of his being was scattered. This was pretty metaphoric if it weren't so shitty. For a guy that retained everything, he didn't remember much this year, his thoughts becoming the brown leaves gusting uncaught in early winter. Occasionally he remembered it being winter, but he couldn't recall fall even if he'd spent the entire last autumn with a rake in his hand.

I missed the service, arriving at the moratorium empty handed. Everyone was milling around waiting, and the stone wall where the urn was to be placed was open like a welcoming door where you could enter a friend's house without knocking. People comfortable with each other would do that.

I remember the days in our courtship when she left the wood door wide open and all I had to do was open the screen. Today I had nothing to offer.

I couldn't even explain what happened in any way that made sense. Seatbelts don't hold urns, and arms cannot wrap a heart up into a hug...as she was there, and people were there, and no one knew what to do or say, but all our hearts were all still beating. Someone should say *something,* so I whispered that to Father David, and he started honoring my father immediately, without a skip, as if he had all the words memorized. Then he shut the door, empty as if Dad never existed. All that was left was the name and date. I stood there until everyone had left for the lunch and it was just she and I.

Touching the inscription, she traced his name without looking at anything but the placard. "I think I'm going to stay down on the Cape for a while." It was as if her door was locked, and the locks changed. The outdoors was lonely, and I was alone with the gusts which blew the thin, barren, branches up and down.

Poke

Wesley was fresh from bouncing around the Internet when he texted his friend Lindy to tell her he had decided to bring poking back.

"Remember when?" he added.

Lindy always thought that poking was strange until she first met her first eventual husband that way.

"Fine. Go ahead," she said, "but don't let me say I told you so after you realize it's 2020."

"It's the pandemic, and people need to be poked!" was his reply.

Wesley had come to this conclusion when logged into social media that morning. He had quit ten months ago, after watching a documentary about why he should quit that platform. He couldn't ever call them by their name either, even when asked if he was on Facebook, he would just answer, "No, I am not on social media." Today he was back because he was bored, but there was a notification that he had been poked over three years ago by someone he didn't know, and if he would like to poke them back.

Wesley was all-in. He returned the poke, and waited. Nothing. That's when he texted Lindy, then weakened after a few when she said to just call her.

"It's like pre-historic Tinder," he said. If you poke someone and they poke back it's like a match, except no swiping.""

"Swiper, no swiping," Lindy said.

"What?"

"Never mind."

"Look," he added. "Those Tinder folks made big bucks. I can too, by bringing poking back, and there's a world of possibilities. I mean an app, just for poking."

"But this already exists," Lindy said. "Also it exists in a way that sometimes, even on Facebook, a poke is just a poke, or just a hello, rather than, you know, a *poke*."

"If you match on Tinder, it's just a match. It's not a fuck."

"Especially, not with you..."

"Shut up," he said.

Wesley went back that night to find people he'd want to poke. In the morning there were messages.

Seriously, a red haired woman one-word replied.

Just trying to bring poking back he wrote back.

Ugh, she messaged...then unfriended and blocked. He wondered how to reinvent this as socially acceptable. He went to old poking history, and poked them all. By morning he had been unfriended 15 more times, and blocked five times. There was one message which said, *Creepy.*

You poked me first, he replied.

Yeah in 2003.

There was also a message from the social media platform informing him his poking privileges had been revoked indefinitely. What??? He appealed. He wrote quickly and concisely in his appeal to Facebook and defined what a poke meant today vs. in 2003. He gave them his plan to come up with a socially acceptable poking app. He went on to describe the success of Tinder and Bumble, and how their own dating app, Datebook, was failing. He even brought up how a poke could open conversation and bring the world closer together.

Wesley logged in every ten minutes to see if his poking ability had been restored. The sun had begun to sink low in the sky until it was under his blinds on his windows. Nothing. At midnight he decided to give it one last try. When he tried to log in he was directed to a page, indicating: *The account associated with this e-mail no longer exists.*

He was pissed, seething even more a month later: Facebook announced to the world that they were introducing their new Pokebook app, which would be automatically installed in all of their platforms, with special new poking emojis. "Fuck Facebook." Wesley yelled. He thought that nearly every time the Face-word came up. Wesley's phone buzzed. A text from Lindy!

"Poke."

Becoming Ice

She dug a shelter in snow, saw the hole in the wall and crawled through into darkness, as the forecast said sunny days and melting ice. That's all it took, hard work and a plan of escape. "I'm leaving him in the cold," she said, slipping out of her ski pants and into cut-offs and a tank top.

That was the easy part. She watched YouTube to learn, "How to Dig a Tunnel," then the video on "Adjusting to a change of Climate: Twelve simple steps." She knew the difference between warm and cold, black and white. The hard part was actually getting out.

A second thought, a few weeks ago: Her lover, her partner in crime, didn't own ski pants. He was ill-equipped. The thoughts of her killing him might kill her.

Yesterday, she threw a snowball through his window as a goodbye before she left. *It will be too sunny for any snow soon,* she thought. Now was the time where she re-entered dark as her unconsciousness. Today, when she peeked into the slit of light, her head banged against a block of ice. She pushed and punched it, attempted to break it into chunks, but it was completely set and stubborn against her. *I'm still stuck*, she thought

Amazon delivered the pickaxe from the town where she left him. She dropped to her knees when she realized the package she chipped at could easily be his frozen body. Then, she swung the pickaxe as hard as she fucking could.

The Retired Poet Bought a Falafel Truck

When the wheels got bald, it was them he re-tired. When he got bald, he wasn't rehired.

What did he do before, when he worked 8 to 4? He saw the future. His name was Paul—an employee without benefits was the extent of it. Not a friend, but younger, took his job. No one wondered.

Making no lettuce, it comes in a head, a bright idea, un-retire instead.

Now cooking with oil, and wrapping things up, the sandwiches silvered with aluminum foil.

When the trucks needs brakes, but he can never get breaks. He works all the time, falls into rhythm.

Suggestions for My Ashes

I don't have any traditional suggestions.

None.

I do not have any orders or wish to tell people what to do with my remains. I know that people grieve. I know there are memories. The best ones they might have with me will be in thoughts and stories and places.

I want no ash spreading ceremony. No gather round, we are going to pour poor Tim back to the earth—like compost! I know there are memories. You will have them, but mine will be done.

When my mother was dying, when she was lucid, she said she wasn't scared. One day she woke up in her hospice room, the first thing she said out of a dream was, "When they cremate you, they don't just throw you in a fire."

I believe dumping out ashes shows about as much care as tossing someone in a fire.

If you have any memoires of me, you should have a piece of me. If it has meaning, take an ash.

One ash?

Sure—minimum. Save some for others that want some, and no one should get the big 'ol urn. Everyone can have a little—I'll be all socialist about it. It's fine. I mean socialism pays for the police and fire. Ashes are from fire, but I digress.

Knowing that everyone has a share is a grand living memory for me. I can imagine someone dropping a little of me over the center field wall at Fenway, onto the warning track. (It's illegal to do this, so carry your small piece of me in your pocket, in a gum wrapper or something...remember no urn). Someone can sprinkle me over Highland Lake in Bridgton, Maine, the way a chef sprinkles parsley on top of a soup. Don't forget live music—you may have a memory with me of that, and I may want to be in the mosh pit—just a little. Or a location...I loved going to Nashville, but look, no pressure, no need to take a trip on my account, after it's all said and done.

Also, maybe a bookstore might host me and put me on a shelf behind some of my books. I could be there a long time...I mean, no one buys books anymore.

But, if you loved me...if you really loved me, you might want to keep a piece of me around the house. You can do that role playing thing when you are alone, and speak into the air, "Oh, Tim, what should I do next?" Just remember, you'll always have my essence, and try not to let me tell you what to do as an ash. Seriously, most of you never listened anyway, so please, don't start now.

And, while I'm there, I'm not watching over you as an ash! Any spiritual guidebook will support that version of the afterlife. An ash is not my afterlife. I'll certainly exist, but not in an Altoid tin.

And, my mom was right.

They won't throw me in a fire.

Because, it is no longer me.

And, I know there are memories.

And, everyone can keep those.

THE SAME CORNER
OF THE BAR

"...as you lose your innocence,
the flower in the vase wilts."
~ 2003 Poems

Sitting drunk on a cooler in my backyard

A warm day in November
A mute butterfly
landed on my arm.

As I decided on whether
it should live or die

It closed
its wings to pray
the last prayer

Arlington Catholic

The petal
in the morning
drips with dew
which can be wiped
away with a light touch
wild and rebellious
you climb on top
hair blown back
by the breeze
of lovemaking.
As you lose your
innocence. The flower
in the vase wilts.

A Do-Dah-Day

I'd like to make a case for boredom
Grass through my toes
A book too heavy on my eyes
The warm earth calling me to nap

And if there is something that
I don't want to think about
Something so terrifying
as the world

today:
let's just drink Lemonade
and call-a-day today
a day

The same corner of the Bar

I sit
waiting
for it...IT
and HER...
or something else.

I see through
boozy evenings
waiting and watching
for IT and HER
or something else
Besides the cold beer
in my mug, friends to the right
laughing and happy
waiting for IT and HER, something else

like Love will walk into this bar
(and it will)
maybe...a funny drunk gal.
We will talk, laugh
into a low hard hug

hip bone against my stomach
her face up close, exquisite,
Her eyes show feelings
until she leaves...
she was IT, HER, SOMETHING ELSE

all rolled into
thirty minutes
of hope caught
in a blink
of my eye.

What were you doing when the Towers Fell?

I saw the twin-towers fall
at Sligo's pub.
Walked in on my way to work
The place was packed
Somehow a crowded bar, at 10 am,
for once, seemed fine.

Insect

I'd love to be a fly on the wall
for that conversation
But instead I am a fly
caught on a no-pest strip
in a dirty old
kitchen in
Mississippi

WE NEEDED
A NIGHT OUT

" ...clutching therapy in a bottle, again."
~ 2005 Poems

My Heart the Car

My heart
has no
backup lights

    this month it needs inspection

My heart
has flashed
its hazards

    disabled in the breakdown lane

My heart
blinks right
blinks left

    doesn't know which way to go

My heart
is beating
in reverse

    flinching, the thought of impact

I may die behind the wheel

Liquid

Walking with a dull ache
an inner limp
that's been there
since boyhood

my gait has swung open
as my hands clinch
my throat opens, clutching,
therapy in a bottle again

Thoughts While Driving

Sometimes while idling
the perfect song comes on the radio
Like you've been waiting for it
Haven't heard it for years
and there it is, sonic youth

It is perfection in basic form
like a stranger's smile
when finding money on the street
like surprised when a soft kiss falling into place
when you don't think too hard about them

Thinking is the problem
a sickness when scripts
re-haunt...re-argue when moving we always
force a large sofa up a small stairwell
It will never give in unless you cut off a leg

Remember
It's stubbing your toe
hearing bad news
those sick minds
I hope not

to wreck this car–
before I hear that song
I hear a voice
a pincushion isn't a pincushion
when you are pushing the pin into a stone

Rorschach while looking at the Clouds

I wonder why dragons blow smoke out their snouts?
Why clowns laugh?
Men chase with knives?
or elephants, Jimmy Durante and
New Jersey appear?

Why do mailman
have to come every day
bringing red notices
with some commitment
made with the weather bureau?

Nothing good can come out of being lonely
looking at the sky, never a woman
American, Red, White
then love to make her blue...
There's never a hundred dollar bill sailing

always
elephants
tugboats
dragons
Jimmy Durante
New Jersey
or clowns

Their nebulous shapes
Indebting and drifting

I Need Enemies

My friends pick me up
and drop me in.
When I'm down

They buy me drinks.
if I have a broken heart
I am drunk nearly everyday

SEVEN

~ for my boy

Today he's seven
and that's about perfect.
He's excited that it's his day
a day that I forgotten

of the innocence myself.
This is going to be the best day ever
for him
for me

He's not old enough
to rebel
to say, "Screw you dad."
because he will because they all will

but today, he's seven.
We wake up
strap in his sister
drive and get pancakes

We party like we're all seven
and that's about perfect, also.

Giving Myself a Haircut

An undaunting task for my stupidity
as I use a clipper on my head
combined with my Attention Deficit Disorder,
it never comes out right.

More than a few times I have to color
some fake hair around my ears with a pencil.
This time the extension to the clipper,
you know, the 1/4, 3/8, 5/16's popped off

as I was ramming the damn thing
into the side of my head,
creating such an obvious bald spot
the deli-man asks me, "How is the treatment going?"

THIS IS WHERE YOU GO WHEN YOU ARE GONE

" ...I've drunk the last slice of apple pie."
~ 2008 Poems

Rabbit Maranville

A baseball bat found
in grandfather's barn
with a signature
Rabbit Maranville
near the barrel

looking ancient
Maranville, Rabbit
on a computer screen
played with a glove
with the pocket cut out
not unlike the hole in palm
of my winter mitten

Rabbit slick in the field
wide-ranging Maranville
spunk and determination
timing. speed, eye-popping
"basket catches."

yet, the name on that bat
was Rabbit Maranville
no silver slugger
never hit a lick
sorry Grampa
it ain't worth shit

I've Drunk The Holidays

I've drunk the sea
the land, the light, my life
and see...drunk
that woman over there

I've drunk the green tufts of growth on the hillside,
the pure soft sound of crashing waves,
Picasso, Doug Henning,
the arms of Venus de Milo

I've drunk the loss of all greatness,
the fulfilling of all prophecies,
every champion or wannabe
and every loser on earth

I've drunk the crafted limestone of Mount Rushmore,
the Great Wall of China,
Arcadia National Park,
a Sphinx or two, drunk

for courtship,
marriage,
divorce,
dating, to death

I've drunk the sun always rising,
the biggest baddest love,
the hunter's lonely heart and
the Magna Carta

I've drunk the last slice of apple pie,
beef stew's slow boil in a crock pot,
the stretch of cheese on chicken cordon bleu,
the sponge in the spinach soufflé

I've drunk J. Robert Oppenheimer,
John F. Kennedy, Fidel Alejandro Castro Ruz,
President Mahmoud Ahmadinejad
and george w. bush

I've drunk bank balances
car payments, VISA,
and Master Card, and all collectors,
the agencies trying save us, drunk,

Winter,
Spring,
Summer,
Fall

I've drunk books, compact discs,
dvds, television,
malls, theater,
computers, sporting events.

Drunk irony,
and Frosty and Rudolph,
and Charlie Brown, and Jimmy Stewart...
damn, drunk, *It's a Wonderful Life*

My Uncle Coming Back from Vietnam with a Stump

Don't stare at it
my father said,
as I thought of trees
that will never grow—
this, the first time
I'd ever experienced
a man's drinking, bitter and quiet,
defeated in battle.

We sat around, I waited for him
to dance and laugh,
like he used to.
Instead, I had to ask
some dumb-ass
brave-hero GI Joe
worship questions—
that never got answered.

Disowned by most of the family

You can't buy your father's car
my aunt told me a few weeks later
'cause when you drive it around
I'll think of him—N-O!

So, I stole the keys,
went for a joyride...
ended up drunk in a ditch,
a turtle on its back.

A small Toyota uproar
for all the rest of them
that would still speak to me
leaving me in a cell

Rotting for the night:
afterward, they gave me some,
"What-da-fuck-were-you-thinking."
"No lessons learned from bailing you out,"

and always final shots,
"Don't be like he was."
backfired from the mob,
the noise rang in my ear.

My aunt, more upbeat, celebrated
a few less things reminding her of her
"asswipe brother", patted me on the back
"You can buy the car now..."

Waking up around noon

While the garbage stays piled in my kitchen
I count the 22 flies I smacked dead
when they parked on my counters and walls
hearing the sharp snap
of the hinged mail-slot
delivering the news of the day:
I can buy two pizzas for nine ninety-nine,
have my cement lot landscaped,
or carpets steam cleaned, cheap

then god calls
to sell me land in Florida
or perhaps to save me
but it's too late,
the dial tone cures my ear,
loudly, I swear
there is no work
in my refrigerator today,
only beer.

reply to someone who said my poems are all sad

fluffy white cotton tail bunnies
pink noses sniff the air
faster than the arc of a rainbow

scurry with sweetness, nuzzling each another,
unconcerned about how cute their existence
is on a rich green hill of grass

even now, sudden is a movement
of a starving wolf creeping, one
whom has not eaten in seventeen months

its hungry saliva corners the bunnies,
who offer their friendship, a paw full of daisies
and dinner of succulent crisp bright carrots

"we are friends of love,"
they all exclaim and giggle,
the wolf even tries to hop.

your personal ground zero
For Franz Wright's writer's block

There are no planes that crash
no one to call us
to where we pray
no, sign of the cross,
for the empty pews
of water damaged wood.

You that the voices were not god
and to get out, stay out, stay damaged,
beaten, crusted and voiceless,
as to believe
what you have left
is a huge undertaking

You see that it's only a personal
small plot of land given you
for the dedication.
Whatever the demons have left you
small on this vacant foundation
it is all you need to start to rebuild.

THESE POEMS ARE NOT PINK CLOUDS

"...the city is bathwater soiled from dirt."
~ 2008 Poems

Hit the road now Jack

the road is holy
smoked straight
worn as the vinyl
of the seat of my dodge...

pick up–
telephone's ringing already
knowing the things
flying by, the pictures in frames

some coffee cups and ashtrays
can ride in the backseat
behind the crash of jazz
played in a time that's broken

Once Upon an Ocean Town

Now, no longer
that I feel this place—

from my wayward friend
to the bluest of oceans
in the hue of her eyes
where I once drove
long and forceful love,
stared deeply—

pushed through your pupils,
the thread from a needle

I loved this woman
once, I stood up
on the top of a hill,
maybe the top of the world
but now, I'm only up there
and searching

On the way home from Maine, 1970

carsick in my father's Beetle,
he uses an ice scraper,
to remove the vomit
from the uncarpeted
floorboard as the voyeur
truckers circle
like the spinning orange orb
of Union 76
Gasoline sign becomes my head
chunks of blueberry mush
from yesterday's Pleasant Mountain buffet
now cook on the pavement
like pancake batter

Summer Job, Concord, Ma.

My first job
was an onion pecler–
garbage dumper,
in the dirty kitchen
of a fish shack
not even on the radar.

One needed to drive
ten miles to find the place
perched on the banks of
a scuzzy green river
where Gerry yelled
at me, the salads weren't crisp

He ignored the other symptoms
such as the painting of a clown
hung in a broken picture frame
in the dank dining room
so, really
what the fuck did I know

telling him the salad would be crisper
if more people ate it...a Catch-22.
He cuffed me hard on the back
of my head, "go do some work, college boy"
he, smart enough to know
the barrels needed to be emptied

Somewhere South

Walk a lonely lane,
where tall trees turn toward
the sun and weeping willows bow,
inviting you to stay
within their succulent shade,
...close your eyes,

dream an ocean
mist moistening your face,
with a cool suave sleep
as veiled voices
echo down dirt roads,
the sounds siphon you awake.

my dear god, we are all so small

you never can anticipate:
brawny men becoming cripples,
humanitarians turning into jerks,
a simple dinner missing the colander
and ending up down the disposal

It's someone's damn fault
there are events as real as these
measured without a yardstick:
like a cat stuck in a tree,
a gravy stain on a white table cloth,
or a house washed away by a flood.
But, the disease growing inside
your friend's body,
was not known
until she vomited, the sickness found,
too late, untreatable.

Now she's down in the ground,
with "so...much...life", fuck
you pour angel hair
into the sink...
it happens that quickly

Night in New York City

god's speed was taken
by us last night, so we walked
across town not caring
how loud we screamed
our mundane thoughts,
as sweat poured from our faces,
the city is bath water soiled from dirt,
we said, strange things,
funny that they won't be remembered
you said, when we hit Broadway
you should lie down here
but never sleep
I said, this is the you I adore,
try to remember *that*

The Things I'd Say

I want to sit on your front steps,
brush my fingers against your bare arms,
their warmth the way sunned cement feels
on the back of our legs,
tell you that I've learned some things:
I'd say I am the captain of a large wooden boat
with a white sail under a grey sky
in a churning dark ocean
and the ocean rocks me
the way a crumpled piece of paper
falls from my desk to the ground.
I know the past is a snapshot;
the future, only imagined

The present, a movie without edits,
which needs to mean something
when shown on the inner-most
screens of our existences.
And when I drank, I drank you forever;
I chugged that love and was never thirsty
but now, I only binge away
hangovers of other lovers--
Today, I wake up tired and thirsty
I also need to tell you I had monsters,
only the size of squirrels, which carried me away.
But I was small myself to let that happen.
Now I have these demons eating peanuts
from the palm of my hand

I remember the hair standing up
on the arm I caressed
how you were right, so right,
in what you gave me
I finally understood,
why things moved on
so I appear here to thank you,
and I miss you–
That you look beautiful
in the picture I put in a frame,
placed on a hard marble mantel
over a burned out hearth.

TREATING A SICK ANIMAL

"...everyone loves a winner."
~ 2009 Flash Fiction

Mangiare per vivere e non vivere per mangiare

My job consists of helping people who are clinically depressed but sometimes I laugh at them when they aren't around. Karma? I've fucked that up pretty good. These past few months I've been more depressed than most the people I have to deal with. It's not like I can't get out of bed, because I can. It's not like I'm weeping in public, because I don't. It's more like things are in slow motion and I'm hungry all the time. When people act that way the worst thing you can say to them is "Why don't you cheer up?" or "It's not that bad". Don't even bother with "Snap out of it" because they can't and they won't. It's the world that has to snap them out of it in some way, creating all the ingredients that cause change.

Let me tell you about a girl. I thought I was in love. We all think that at some point, right? Love actually sticks when it's right, the same way that pasta does—you throw it against the wall and see if it's good. In college I had a white-tiled wall in my kitchen that was loaded with crusty hard pasta. I had a lot of lovers in college and I ate a lot of pasta. I was a pasta stud way back when. But the big question remains: What happens when it doesn't stick after you thought it was perfect? You might decide to go hungry. That's what I did.

I recently wrote a novel I didn't finish. It was called *After my Funeral I wanted to Kill Myself*. It was about the afterlife. Ironically it focused too much on the funeral and the character's life before that, but it never got that involved with the actual afterlife. It was a bad idea. There was an early chapter about the main character not being afraid of dying, but later, there were too many chapters about him being afraid of living. I stopped writing it after he died. There was nothing else to write about.

OK, here's a snap out of it moment: A grasshopper walks into a bar and the bartender says, "We serve a drink named after you." The grasshopper looks at the bartender and says, "You have a drink named Steve?" Funny, right? It's the easiest thing in the world to not be a round-hole. And that girl I was telling you about, the round peg? She left me stranded in the desert after shooting out three of my tires. She looked fine walking away. It was only then that I moved on.

Hidden Hoboken

Vince knew by the hanging chips of paint and the cracks in the window that Sinatra never lived here yet the owner obviously wanted to work that angle. "So you going to take the place or not?" the owner asked. Vince noticed his way of gesturing loudly every time he spoke. Sharon hung on Vince's arm. "Vince...we gonna take it? Come on...Sinahhhtra, the King of the Hill, Cream of the Corn, A-Number One, la-dee, da-dee, dee."

Sharon looked at Vince kind of cockeyed when she drank too much and it was one of those times again as her hand worked constantly sweeping the wispy hair out of her eyes. She pulled on his sleeve and whispered loudly. "It's so romantic. It's Sinatra's house. He slept here, he walked here on these floors." Vince released himself from her grip and walked the room himself. He walked from dusty corner to dusty corner. "Why's it been empty so long?"

"Restoration," the owner added dragging his tongue over the chip in his front tooth, "you're not going to rent a place like this in Hoboken for $1300, with its historic value and all."

"Yeah there's *Sinatra* historic history in this house," Sharon chirped as Vince mumbled something.

History *was* here in Hoboken in the era of Old Blue Eyes. Men worked the docks, lived in the factories; barely came home to eat and more often out for drink. Hoboken, their Hoboken, was the worst of times, the bottom of the barrel; the pool halls, the "set 'em up Joes" and the abuse of the Big H. That horse came into the city a little later between that time and this time. Now, Hoboken is a city in revival.

"This is cheap, no?"

Vince wouldn't answer. "What was his name again?" Sharon whispered to Vince.

"Bobby Marshall," the owner answered. "You gonna take the place or what? What are you..."

"I heard it was destroyed by fire," Vince cut in.

Bobby pushed his hand nervously down the front of his shirt. "Yes, I may be from out of town, but I do know a little history. Sinatra's house was destroyed by fire."

"Ya mean he never lived here?" Sharon asked.

"Of course he lived here," Bobby quickly snorted. "After. He lived here after." He turned to Vince. "So you know a little history?"

"I know some. I know enough."

"So then what do you want to do?"

"First, I think the rent should be cheaper. About $900 would be a fine place to start."

"He didn't live here?" Sharon voice muted.

"900..."

"Sure if you wish to discuss this in private," Vince said. "Let's say we go to the basement. We are allowed in the basement, aren't we?"

Bobby wiped the sweat from his top lip, and his shirt wet enough to form a dark colored outline of New Jersey on the chest of his blue t-shirt.

"Come on, let's take a walk" Vince said to Bobby. They went into the other room. "Of course the basement is open to you," Bobby said. "The place is clean. Shit, I was cleared of that...found NOT guilty. You heard that, right?"

"You think no one watches Court TV. Give me $400 off just because every day I'll think about what was hidden in that basement. OK? Do we got a deal?"

Bobby rubbed his hand on his dungarees. "Deal. $900 for the historic value."

Vince bounded back into the room where Sharon was looking up at the tattered ceiling.

"We're going to take it," Vince said.

"It needs some work," she said.

"Yes, but he lived here, Sharon. He lived here."

Your Vasectomy Journal

Do it because neither of you wants children ever again.

It's really an easy decision because you've been dating for six months and have absolutely talked about it. The two of you are in love, but mistakes happen, and getting pregnant would be a huge one. You're forty-six, have two children, and she's younger with one, but both of you are barely able to handle the kids you have. At this point, you do not want to be the parent with a walker playing catch with your nine-year-old. Tony Randall fathered children later in life, and now he's dead. You make an appointment to see a specialist.

Screaming is not an option, Part 1.

When the doctor grabs your vas deferens and shakes it around with what looks to be a tool that strips copper wire, it feels like she's playing a drum solo on your balls. You're a baseball fan, but you try not to think of Chris Snyder, the Diamondbacks catcher who suffered a broken testicle from a foul tip. It is likely—no, it is very definite—that, in the waiting room, your girlfriend can hear you groaning and yelling. "Perhaps we didn't give you enough pain killers," the nurse says.

Masturbate twenty-five times or wait six weeks
to get rid of all potentially active sperm.

Those words are the instructions found in your Personal Discharge Summary. Six weeks? In reality, it takes eight days. Twenty-five times? You do it thirty, just to be safe.

You really want to try out your new junk, and the thought of waiting the entire six weeks with the same old pre-procedure sexual practice is torturing you. You make an appointment with the lab to drop off the sample. The sperm container looks kind of like the side of mayo you get at the deli down the street. "Thank you," you say to the woman in the white lab coat. "Have a nice day."

Shoot without guilt.

You're going to do it, and it's going to be wonderful. You're going to push your entire package inside her, as far as it can possibly go, into a galaxy of pleasure you've never been before, and you will be able to shoot with so much force she'll feel it in her lungs. There will be no pulling out. There will be no perfect attempt at targeting the stomach with semen when 99 percent of the time it ends elsewhere. Your dick is not accurate, much like a garden hose held four feet from the end. Today, you can shoot-shoot-shoot-shoot. And you will score.

Screaming is not an option, Part 2.

Calmly ask the lab what you should be doing before bringing in the next sample, since they just told you that you have a sperm count. "That's impossible," you say. "I was way over the twenty-five ejaculations. Do I need to do more?" This question sounds ridiculous, especially when said with a wavering voice. "It's only a guideline," the lab person says on the other end, "but this time, wait for the results. Just to be safe."

Buy a home pregnancy test.

These results only take four minutes--about the same time it takes to listen to Duane Eddy's "Rebel Rouser." One pink line in the kit's window, with one blank, means negative; a single pink line in both windows means positive. You see two pink lines in her test, and you reread the brochure. The information isn't sinking in, so you have to look at the picture on the tri-folded paper for full confirmation that the two distinct lines mean she's actually pregnant.

Consider your future.

Your future is a blessed irony. You consider naming the baby Iron, middle initial E. She and you have a few laughs at that one, but, after three weeks, the idea of becoming a dad again has grown on you. A new phase of your relationship, one with a baby, is beginning—plus, you're in love. You think about the future and what town you want to live in together. You think about the timelines; when the new baby is a certain age, how old will the rest of them be? You lie in bed with your arms around her, thinking these peaceful thoughts.

Screaming is not an option, Part 3.

She wakes up and there is blood. She has lost the baby, and there is nothing you can do. You want to fix it but you can't. Trying again can't be considered, so you can't ever make this up to her. You can't make it up to yourself, either. Somehow, the blame shifts. You never wanted a baby, but now you are full of loss.

Break up because she really did want children.

You never thought it would end like this. She tells you it's fine because you're remaining true to your decision to never have children, and that you should be happy with that. She says it's not you, it's her. You have opened her heart to having children again, and now that's no longer possible with you. Sometimes, things happen for the best. She smiles when she says that.

Punchless Jimmy Collins

"Punchless" Jimmy Collins has a scar over his right eye, a crooked nose and an ear that bobs when he walks. In his prime, his "punchlessness" beat opponents but never knocked them out. Often he left the ring a warrior, teetering like a wounded dog, the crowd cheering. Everyone loves a winner.

He is fifty-five, his robe is ragged and he needs a shave. The nurses have stopped paying attention to the sound of his left palm banging the side of his head, slapping away the ringing. Ironically, he is completely deaf in his right ear.

Every month when the bell rings Jimmy refuses to evacuate and returns to the ring once more, a 10 by 15 foot room with windows that won't open. He lashes out, fists against air.

"Mr. Collins! It's a fire drill," the attendant shouts.

"I'm fine, I'm fine," he counters, popping his dentures in and out of place.

"FI-AH drill," Hugo replies.

"Hold onto your towel," Collins snaps.

Hugo has a towel tucked into his belt, not to concede a fight, but rather to clean up messes at SunRich.

"Sonny, leave that towel alone!" Collins threatens.

"Champ. My name is Hugo. Remember? Hugo." Sonny was his cut man. The best in the business. "Champ, the fights over," Hugo says.

"Over?'

"Yes, You won again Jimmy! Now step down, the limo is waiting downstairs."

They turn and leave, Hugo, behind him, holding his shoulders as they both bounce down the hall. Outside,

Collins brushes past the gathering crowd, strangely quiet after a big fight.

Jimmy Collins Jr. visits twice every month. He is the only one and comes here because he can't take care of him out there. "Pop, remember this one?" he asks while pointing to an old newspaper clipping in a tattered scrapbook.

"Oscar Bonavena," he said.

"No, Pop, that's Bugner. How about him?"

"Bonavena."

"Um, that one is Mike Quarry. Jerry's brother. He waits, turns the page. Here's one you know."

"Oscar Bonavena." It was Bonavena on the last page of the book. "Where's Mary?" Punchless Jimmy Collins asks.

"Mom's gone Pop. Been gone a while." The fighter glazes over as if he was badly hurt, a slow dance during a final round. He winces as jabs and uppercuts connect in his brain.

"She left you Pop. You smacked her pretty good. You don't remember."

Collins never responds, barely hanging on to an angry blur of Mary leaving each day, until the day she is no longer there.

He will wake up soon, a referee or trainer looking down on him. Sometimes it is a nurse or sometimes it's Sonny.

"Mary's dead?" Punchless Jimmy Collins asks and then the bell rings again.

The Top of Grace's Upper Lip

I hate the situation I am in. I hate my house. It is too big. Cleaning it is dirty work but someone has to do it and that someone is me. I wish it is as easy as kissing the leftover tomato sauce off top of Grace's upper lip.

It is a long day at the hospital for Grace and sometimes it's a long night. It depends what shift she is on. Me? I'm gainfully unemployed, but you'd think, it would be peaches and cream doing what I do. Don't get me wrong, I'm not your typical castrated stay at home male; as I am not a televisionally depressed kind of guy. There are things around the house that can challenge me even in the simplest ways. First, off the top of my head, I take pride in my laundry. The goal here is to catch the timing for the fabric softener, otherwise you need to restart the rinse cycle so everything will feel and smell just right. Grace likes to look and smell good when she goes to work. Also, big secret, I take pride in my food shopping. Cost is not an issue. I know there is money on our debit card. Trick is to buy everything on sale at the end of each aisle and the rest takes care of itself. Grace says, "If I were no longer with you on this earth, you'd have enough pasta for the rest of your life." True. Pasta is always on sale and we have pounds of it. Grace's hair twirls like cavatappi.

Grace tells me she has a difficult time trusting people. Grace tells me she is a slave for her schedule. Grace tells me not to keep track of her schedule because it's creepy. Grace tells me she can do better than me. Grace tells me she wonders when the last time I used the vacuum. Grace works too hard. Grace gets angry.

Grace works a few days a week at 7 AM, a few at 3 PM and the rest on the overnight shift. It is exhausting. I am exhausted. I look in the mirror and I have bags under the bags under my eyes. I must put a good meal in her when she comes home. I cook and I cook and I cook. I cook well and she eats. Sometimes she is too tired to eat but she eats anyway. Sometimes...she thanks me. I like the way she holds her fork. It is dainty, yet forceful. She is the same way in the sack or I should say she was that way in the sack. I don't know about that now as we only sleep in the sack. I try to adjust everything so that things remain harmonious between us. Sometimes I take sleeping pills to sleep when she sleeps. Sometimes things are only the way things are.

She ends a lot of shifts at 7 AM. She is working extra. There are more patients and the nurses have a crappy contract. That is fine as she is sorry. She is sorry she can't spend the extra time but the money will help us. The money is good in theory, but there is things that start to confuse me. Things suddenly pop up. This is what pops up at the grocery store: Our checking account isn't as free and easy as it was a few months ago. I have to whip out a credit card two weeks in a row to cover the uncomfortable moments at the checkout line and then, on the way home, as I think of the savings I made on Tide this week, there is an epiphany. It is as clear as the word "Declined" I witnessed a few moments ago. There is something that won't add up no matter how many times I crunch the numbers. It is something I think she finds in the arms of someone else between 11 P and 7 A.

My house *is* now bigger. Cleaning it is dirty work but someone has to do it and that someone is me. I wish it is as easy as kissing the leftover tomato sauce off top of Grace's upper lip. I just wish.

Just Dessert

Fiddling with your buckle I say, "It's big. Are you a pilgrim?" You exhale the essence of Lamb Vindaloo we ate hours earlier, your stomach now rising and falling like bellows. It was then, at dinner, you laughed about us eloping, but as long as we did so after dessert. You were the one, too stuffed to order rice kheer, so I just threw that marriage thing away. Are you kidding me? Now, help me with this belt of yours, I think we can be happy.

The Short Marriage of a Bride and Groom

All I wanted to do was run but my patent leather footwear sank into the frosting. I was the guy wearing a tuxedo smiling on top of the wedding cake. My wife joined me there on the happiest day of our lives. Things went wrong the second they sliced into the cake. Imagine being in an earthquake and having the world open up in front of you. Would you be able to run? You'd think someone might have prepared me; given me a talking to or purchased me a set of snowshoes.

My wife stood there, a smile painted on her face, her dress hard and unmoving. It was the sign of things to come as on our wedding night when I tried to take that dress off it would not budge. Talk about frustrating. For hours I attempted to remove that dress. I'd been stiff all day but now when it counted I couldn't even get a decent hump out of it. She was sexless. She didn't move. Plastic.

That set the stage for the beginning of our new life together. We spent a lot of it lying around. I realized now that we never spoke, never even left the house. After a few years we became removed from one another. My friend told me he saw her on top of another cake.

I often feel used and forgotten now. I've been left at the bottom of a utility drawer which rarely gets opened. Maybe my dream girl will someday find me laying with the coupons, paperclips, ten dozen pennies, the back-up to the back-up corkscrew and a refrigerator magnet from a closed auto repair shop. When she does, I'll know what to do beyond the top of a cake.

EXPERIENCE, STRENGTH, AND HOPE

~ 2012 Essay

Experience, Strength, and Hope

November 6, 2010

I'm coming out of a blackout at The People's Republik in Cambridge, Massachusetts and I'm in mid-sentence. I know where I am because I remember coming in with some friends earlier. I can never leave early enough. I confused where this sentence is going to or even what I am talking about. I don't know where my friends I came with are? Did they leave me here? Why? Stupid question because I know even if I wasn't remembering specifics of this night. Bad behavior leads to lost friendships.

How do I get home? Oh, that's right, I remember I drove here. How did they get home? I'm sure they did. They're able to as most people are when they go out. Shit, where is my car? I walk out of the bar. Damn I don't know the answer to that car question. I'm on Massachusetts Avenue and there are various public parking lots nearby. I'll go to each one. My car is a blue Dodge Caliber. Easy enough. I go to each lot and it takes over an hour, mostly because I'm running from one lot to another. I find the car of my friends. They are still in Central Square somewhere. I feel panicked until I find my own car, then I feel like finding my vehicle is some sort of miracle. I start the car, poke my face with the ends of my fingers for sore spots. None. No one has hit me tonight. I turn the key.

I've driven drunk too many times. At least four times per week. I've driven drunk with my children in the car. I've drank beer out of a cooler with my children in the car. I've driven blacked out and greyed out. I'm eventually going to kill myself doing this. I get home I think I do want to kill myself but I want to live. I just don't want the pain. I go through the mental checklist: gunshot, pills, cutting my wrists, jumping off a building. It is how I got to sleep every night, meditating on this list, except tonight I don't sleep. I run the list in my head over and over again without passing out. I'm tired of not wanting to live. At 6 AM, I move to the sofa in fetal position under a comforter.

The position of a fetus strikes me as being pretty claustrophobic. I'm feeling that fear. My temples pound, my vision is pixelated when I try to focus on anything. I do not want to move. My friends hate me. Bad behavior leads to lost friendships and lost relationships. I know this. My last relationship was with a woman with six years sobriety. I told her that I was a social drinker. When we started sleeping together it was the three of us: Me, her and a bottle of Johnny Walker. She broke up with me. I remember she went to meetings. She used to leave my house for a few hours to attend and then come back later.

I tried attending meetings once years ago. Maybe, I didn't but here's the story: I called a hotline for help and they didn't help me on the spot. I went to a bar and got home and my roommate told me that there was a call from them and I told him that it was a wrong number. That about summed up previous ability to surrender.

So at 7 AM, I suddenly remembered that this woman had gone to meetings on Saturday in Needham, the next town. I dragged myself to my computer, did a search and I found it. I envisioned her being there and somehow nursing me back to health—a sober, in recovery, Florence Nightingale. It was in nine hours till the meeting, if only I could hold on.

How It Used to Work

Drinking was great and I was good at it. I was attracted to it as early as age seven when I tried to drink vanilla extract. In high school, it helped me to invent myself as something I was not because I was an awkward, uncomfortable, unconfident, picked on and extremely "uncool" person. So I became this person that partied a lot and stood out as someone that didn't do things in a conventional way. I played in a band, which fueled my drinking, drug taking and womanizing fire. When people guessed I may have a drinking or drug problem and they had the courage to tell me, I was more likely to celebrate that fact than to try to fix it. At least, I was getting noticed. My parents even bought me *A Drinking Life* by Pete Hamill, and I was disappointed that it wasn't pro-drinking. That's how I identified with alcohol as a solution.

That was then...

I wrote my first collection of stories, *Twenty-Six Pack*, in 1999, which I felt was celebrating those certain aspects of my life, but when I look back on it, it reads like a dark drunk-a-log. It turned out to be more of a message about the bad spaces you end up in when using, then anything else.

Then things started going worse. Normal people were settling down and I was still out there. When you hit early to mid-thirties you should no longer act and get wasted like you were ten years younger. It's the difference between college binge alcoholism which I could get away with and the adult progressive disease which was taking over and taking full power over me for another fifteen years. I had no control over it and the moments which I did, I chose it.

Year One

Month one was punishment. I punished myself for the sins of my past. I attended five-seven meetings a week. I missed alcohol and ran to a meeting instead of a bar. I hated every minute of it and I was out of my head crazy. I hadn't killed anyone. I hadn't been fired. I hadn't gone to jail or rehab. I was divorced but drinking of course, wasn't the cause but it presented an excuse to drink more. All I knew was that in the winter of 2010, I didn't want to drink anymore, so I accepted my punishment and began attending AA regularly. When I received my one month chip, I whispered to the presenter, "I don't think I can do this," to which she said, "I think you can."

The second month was bad but better than the first. My head started to clear and the purpose of me staying sober became stronger. I was still in mourning for my "loss" but the days were just better enough for me to understand why I was doing what I was doing. At the three month mark, it was like a switch had been turned on and I was felt lighter. It was only ninety days, many of them bad, but one at a time. I could do that. I was happy about my decision and by month four, I was all in.

Along with my new purpose being strong, memories and emotions started to flood back. They told me that I was indeed like others in the rooms. I had been fired from jobs. My music career basically ended when two very popular bands had given up on me because of how

I drank and used. I had spent a few nights in jail because of fighting while being under the influence. I drove my car many times into guardrails and curbs. Somehow I compartmentalized that those incidents hadn't count. I now realized how I justified a lack of responsibility and accountability during that those times.

I continued to be comfortable and happy with what I was doing to stay sober. I set up chairs for a 5 PM meeting nearly every Tuesday and Thursday. The meeting couldn't exist without me. I became known and acquainted with people with long time sobriety. I also ran with a pack of four people who were all new and were willing to support each other. All of us successfully received our medallions after one year of sobriety.

Life Up To Now

It is better. I accept myself. I am there for others. I am there for myself. Meetings are necessary but not desperately so as there are enough tools I've picked up that I can live life on life's terms. I keep it simple, but incidentally, as simplicity now happens as a norm. My life IS simple and I realize that events happen regardless, whether good or bad and I can handle them without turning to outside substances. I have fought and continue to fight a disease. I've written a book of poetry about recovery. I finished a novel. My children are no longer scared of me. I'm in a relationship with another sober person. I use the steps as a solution and I will continue to work at these. People say they are inspired by me when they decide to start their own journeys. I had my last drink November 6, 2010, my name is Tim and I am sober today.

ANTI-SOCIAL
NETWORK

"Put on Miles Davis if you're not sleeping..."
~ 2013 Poems

Mid-Life Diner

There's this place
where omelets salted with butter
taste perfectly
blessed in ham and peppers
the same way the jazz of
Miles Davis' spangled
notes during Almost Blue
are best listened to
'round midnight
in the spot I'm at, baby
open all night.

It's a slight interruption
from the gossamer
of the American dream
which is what we talk about
these days, monies and marriages lost
like bamboo twigs
in a tsunami's distempered thrashing
replaced by split-second
glimpses of an entrance,
high-heels clicking on a dirty
green and white checked floor.

So here's a toast
to your mouth
slathered bright red
lips of jelly,
a proposed bailout
when butter meets jam.

Like the Moths in the Night

thoughts of suicide
enter, like dirt shoveled
onto my chest
Don't push it off
my friends are heavy

One said I saved them
in dark periods; one
never saw their hands
in front of their face when
there was a full moon

they never looked up
but for my very best friend
it was too late and he rests in the ground
the worst part (that day I gave up on not drinking)
was trying—but that was a long time ago.

Tonight, the outside air is cool
I feel his noose tighten
when I breathe,
and her needle
leaving a bruise

I feel his brains
blown out, like mine
splattered into the universe
for them, why not
me? I haven't the guts.

I sit on a porch
on a summer night
keeping the lights off
because there is nothing
at all in that.

The Enabler

I'm having premonitions of death
which manifested last week in
lying in bed thinking about my own.

I know. It's not going to be me,
but I feel something coming,
something so horrible that I'm afraid

to say anything to anyone,
even if it's about weather.
My thoughts tell me that

when it rains,
things get wet.
I know what water is.

As a boy, I'd place my ear on train tracks.
When I heard the vibration I ran.
becoming deaf and slow.

Now distance is too close.
I still can see you
lying on the tracks

when I pay for the ticket,
trains move quicker.

April Ends

Now, there are May flowers
blooming out of my bald spot
from April where I lost my umbrella.

These are the truths to be told—
not the ones to cover up, like
schizophrenia runs in my family

(I try to hide that from my therapist)
what good would that do, she'd pick
daffodils from my head, plant them in her vase,

say to me they didn't exist. I won't reveal
the scars I had in early March from the lion,
or the case of mint jelly I ate later that month either.

It left a good taste in my mouth, unlike
the new prescription she ripped from her book
trying to take the spring from my step.

Recipe for a Great Poem

For the poet Kenneth Clark

Start with food. Describe how
it simmers in some broth

whiskey or beer then place me
in a chair ready to eat,

fork prongs dug in, juices coming out
from a firm jab by strong hands.

Add in a woman next to me
in a slatted wooden chair.

Create warm conversation.
Let her dress ride up

as she laughs
breasts noticeable

when reaching down
for a glass of wine, then

bring it all to a slow boil after
adding her as seen through

the dress's thin fabric
caught in the sunlight

but please, a slight pinch
of sadness. Stir in some

yearning
for the last time.

Some despair—let it cook
for a long, long time.

Ode to the Wormwood

Growing on roadsides and wasted places
the wormwood braces itself against wind,
remains strong, please, there is a fierce poison
here, the water will be polluted, the
drink held in your hand, downed fast with eyes closed,
resting on the passage in the Bible:

> *"and the third part of the waters became*
> *wormwood and many men died of the waters*
> *because they were made bitter."*

Such is the way of real exterminates,
ridding people of the pests found within
the demise of souls, other flowers that die,
in the ruins of such allowances,
we all try to fight—severe bludgeoning
from these killers, such foul, foul addictions.

I love you wormwood, so misunderstood
defiant, dear life, near death, it suits you,
the sanctuary, so clear is the symbol
here, the water will be polluted, the
drink held in your hand, downed fast with eyes closed,
resting on the passage in the Bible.

Funeral With No Music

You know my dad was dead or dying
when my dog was dead or dying
so sudden she expired in my arms that
Sunday I was ill prepared to start the hole,
so I sat and paced, then slept till Monday.

It was me that drove the golf cart
to under the Jane Magnolia tree.
Lady's matted body teetered as
the Hefty Bag crackled in the wind;
her tail stuck out of it.

None of this:
the flowers red-purple on the outside,
white on the inside,
smelled sweet, after
I sat there, my hair layered in sweat,

the shovel caked with dry dirt,
thinking dad deserves
to die alone, the amount of times
he cocked a gun to his head
fucking with all of us.

His funeral can be silent for all I care
just like the quiet I found in one
of the great discoveries of my childhood,
when I escaped to his back yard
to taste the small drops of honeysuckle.

When It is Still Winter

My Valspar sailcloth walls
against the snow
on the windowsill
needed a coat
of new paint.

Your tracks on my front walkway
are now covered so clean—
You left when it was falling,
perhaps you were never here
but I know you've visited

a hundred thousand times
this morning;
like a faint song
I heard birds singing
of springtime.

at eleven-fifty-nine

put on Miles Davis
if you're not sleeping
or nothing not...milling around
on your notes.
what are we

anyway, there are times
we say we care about
each other far away
drifting...drifting...
in and out of love,

we do this
as empty people do.
the pillow says
sink, quit, when it talks—
it's only talk

ESSAY: A BIT ON THE BOMBING

~ 2013 Essay

A Bit On The Bombing

I live in Boston. I love Boston but it was a slow courtship for me as I grew up in New York and went to college in Delaware where basically I crashed and burned. Given that, Boston is now my beloved town but somehow it didn't feel that anything took place in Boston yesterday. Let me explain. The marathon bombing did not feel real to me, as it felt it could have happened anywhere. One week ago, I was at the Boston Public Library, right near the site of the bombing participating in a reading. My mind today does not connect last weekend and yesterday. Yesterday seemed like a movie, a video game set in my town, yet the setting was a perfect one for an act such as this, as there was no way this tragedy could be prevented with the millions of folks placed at an event such as this, without tickets, or turnstiles. Yet it still seemed not to be Boston to me, as I hurt for humanity in every city, not just here.

At the moment, here are the facts: Two bombs went off. There is no known terrorist group taking responsibility, no know suspects, or no known motive. Our news outlets would like to guess at groups or motives. Our citizens who now have access to places like twitter and facebook would like to become news outlets. News outlets such as the NY Post would like to sell papers and report sensationally. As this was playing out the reports were rolling in about terrorist groups, men on roof tops, captured suspects, other bomb sites including JFK Library and a Rhode Island bus station. Reports of victims ranged from 50 to 2. Want it or not, all of this is falls within the abysmal age we live in.

Yet, as I watched three news stations on television simultaneously, this was what I was seeing/reading on facebook/twitter. One person even commented "Yes!"

under an under-sourced article the NY Post rushed up, which said they have a Saudi being guarded in a hospital because they were a suspect. The Post's main bullet points were 12 dead, suspect named and JFK Library was the site of a third detonated bomb. All three of these points are now being viewed as incorrect. There was no, "No!" posted as the facts rolled in.

What was not in the news? The possibility of a single deranged bomber. Didn't something like this happen 18 years ago in Oklahoma City? Hadn't there been numerous singular gun welding terrorists attacking us every few months or so without real motive or reason beyond what was in their twisted skulls? Sure.

My main point here, rather than give my opinion or guess at facts and motives, has more to do with reporting and gullibility. We are all reporters in our own right. The news and media have certain checks or at least they used to but we should all be checking ourselves on facts and sources before we bring information out to the foreground. What happened yesterday made me sick and angry--and the weird and invalid posts, only misinform or fan the fire of fear. This leads to some serious opinion taints and real world outcomes.

Take this for example; a more minor outcome. People want to help so they post "please give blood". Sounds nice, right, except for one thing. The police, Red Cross and Boston city leaders were all stating because of safety and blood supply, NOT go into Boston to give blood; they were all set, yet this information was getting out there. Should those informed post "no" and the reasons under all these posts. I would have except it felt like strange, nearly asshole-like behavior, to waste time correcting people when terrible things were happening.

Maybe we can learn from this, as the reporting from this evolving tragedy is far from over. The sorrow today will quickly switch to retaliation, especially if it is proven that there is a group associated with this bombing. The posts I'll read will be, "let's get them" or "make them pay!" and at all costs. This I can predict, as I've seen it time and time again. We must remember, that the brave soldiers and patriots that enlisted after 911, who signed on for revenge and protection, who honestly, and bravely served didn't get what they signed up for. I hope to not see that again and I hope that we as human beings with a voice use a little bit of restraint and a little less hysteria as this plays out in the next few days and longer.

As for my feeling toward Boston, I mean, Anywhere, USA. We will recover, we won't forget but we must form careful and valid points of view during and after all of this sifts out. It is our responsibility to take in the news, and form educated opinions but we must remember that we are not the news, we are not the attention grabbers or the center stage ring masters. In events such as this, we sure as hell should not ever be.

THE
SHUTTING DOOR

"We are solid oak doors that shut on our past..."
~ 2013 Poems

Walking Out of the Woods

there's a condom and ten suboxone
in the inside jacket pocket
but I won't use

either

it's been awhile
or there's a tree
standing in the

forest

gracefully not falling
except, through the branches,
there is brilliant

blue

look up,
god.
look up.

I have mostly Nightmares

You curl against me
the coastline, I wake to

your calf, it left a wrinkle
in my comforter;

a note; a funnel cloud,
destroyed everything,

you left the foundation,
the coffee maker brewing.

The Shutting Door

We are solid oak doors that shut
on our past, close on dead mothers,
sons, daughters. These doors swell
often, won't open. One midnight

we walked towards woods, the moss
cold under our toes, as we were,
caught in the light for a moment;
a glimpse of half full. We are dim

lights on dark nights, sending out calls
to the wolves howling at the sun
because the moon hanging there,
yet never seems to hear them.

If I should need to step back to see
how you glow in this light,
illumination, I can be at one with that,
us, growing like violets in the dark

Missteps

When I raised my hand
told a gray room the reasons
I started drinking, I wanted
 to start again immediately.
Told people, whose faces looked like
The End of the World, the truth.

Then I told them I would pour a girl
I'd lusted after, down like whiskey,
her lovely legs spread
until they snapped,
so I could feel like I used
her, an orgasm, I gulped,

running down my neck
like streams of veins.
Oh, I said I never used dope,
when I asked her for it, nicely,
she said, No, she would never

give it up, just got up, waltzed
out of my life. So I begged:
Please, God, stay with me tonight,
here in this church basement.
Please, I can't picture heaven.

You Knew Me Before

I was reincarnated
from an animal, a snake,
a pig, then lastly a bear.

You said you saw me
walking to the stream
pulling out raw salmon
with my teeth, jaws clenched,

sinking into the soft pink;
the spray from their guts
misted my face while I devoured
fermented berries until I laid

legs up, full bellied sleeping
in the sun after I roared,
raved, destroyed everything I touched,
my clothes wrinkled, shoes untied—

Remember how I held a knife and fork
like a hammer and chisel?
Look how I created something
beautiful out of rock.

The poems at my house

My children are more than only words, rolled
together or random specks of dust flying
through amber light. It seemed fuzzy,
how they turned in flight to butterflies?

I wanted out of there. I'll stay
the caterpillar, I cannot change
the way my children leaned
over paper plates, ate watermelon,

the red juice ran down their bare legs,
spat out the seeds, as if they were
dirty things rising in an arc,
as far as they could go. Each moment

held it's sunlight on the lawn,
where my daughter ran,
thought poems were wishes
blown on dandelions,

"Be happy," she said,
handed me the limp stem
like a gift, or an obligation,
"Here."

Meeting with Father Vincent

"Can you grasp the music of a thousand Gods?
I can," says Father Vincent. "False," is all I hear,
the aggregate of everyone's decomposition.

I believe in rusty trucks, feral cats and orphans.
People die for no reason, inherent wickedness
knows no spirit. The stone straight pastor tells me,

"There is hope in the unknown. I know,
we all decay in the ground, the same way,
then we're dust." I can't get a handle around that;

I don't carry a broom at all times. I am there,
a part of the "us." I believe in killer storms.
he says, there's no faith worse than death.

Trouble is, I can't believe in God without
swallowing pills. Men of the cloth have no idea,
what I can take; it's nothing they can prescribe.

When you live by Yourself

You can bench press
your weight in quietness
gets so you talk to your cats
but they won't say
"I love you," back.

You listen to the world
through those feeling-sorry-
for-myself songs, you wish
you never played
over and over again.

CHIEF JAY STRONGBOW IS REAL

"After your leaving, the Hungry Man
was pulled out of the microwave."
~ 2017 Poems

Throw Certainty Out in the Air like a Lasso

Reflections on Alton Sterling

Hatred is a deafening siren
warnings of a terrible twister

out there, it's only one. Earth
tilled by a machine We need topsoil,

moisture, fertilizer to grow a single weed
left bent. Throw questions out in the air

like a lasso. Shady, when the closed rope
loosened, it's what we know of the truth.

Didn't See it Before I Stepped in it

After my Dodge sat in flood water,
After it miraculously started,
After the floorboard dried,
The car still smelled of the dog turd
I'd stepped in last November.

After I drenched it with Fabreze
After I sprayed OdorGone
After I sneezed for days
After it all
after the afters.

After the excuses After all votes
I pretend , this presidency
is kind of "earthy"
After the rain I am
driving this car like a boat.

Prayer By a Stream

God, I've sat on my knees,
in the slowing brook,

brackish tributaries. I'd hoped
the muddy banks could hinder

the deluge unfolding
if only, I could drink

the years pinched tight.
Slackening, you leave me

waving at the sky,
curling into a sore spot

beneath the broken frames,
the branches sliver, providing

leaves painted, subtle ground
voices: *isn't there a better place?*

Sobriety

It can exist
drink coffee

milk, three sugars,
stirred with a straw.

Sit on the sofa,
legs curled under

view the oil paintings
hung boats and fields

thousands of brush strokes
thousands.

How We Exist

The confrontation
between water and blacktop
is elegant, how we exist,
like wash and refuse,
down a street splashed clean.
Our lives flush us out,
the hush unleashed
faintly out to sea...

In the end, it's pouring,
not letting up, please
let me compose myself
quick, it's just that
the sound of the thrashing,
by rain into my core
is a muse in the flood.
By no means stop.

This is where I Am (when here)

after your leaving, the Hungry Man was
pulled out of the microwave, telling me
you won't ever come back, you gave

a homeless man ten dollars once,
to make his eyes glimmer
but when I walked passed

today I identified and wished
him well, I meant no harm, no foul
odor, no one remembers, how I sent

bad advice, if you have a migraine,
use a pistol or a baseball bat, I lie
in this bed, this cold vacant head

wonders about empty, hallow, homes;
times when they were not that bad,
yet, I just can't help I'm at this place.

A Poem For Forever

this light touches like one from a fireplace
sits in the sky too, an orange sunset
paints the far edge of the world

limitlessness He'll take you
never without permission—
        you know God

create Him
a sweeping gate of untainted joy,
You made eternity, knowledge

        Love,
the transmission, You are
        All

Family, friends
chant it, think it, are
It, resending faith

symbiotic—ecstasy
not of this world.
You no longer wait

        Just receive;
        be.

Unfit Father

My children made me lose my head,
today at the beach, my patience

vanished like waves taking turns,
retracting back to the ocean.

I'm tied to their hindrance,
never to sail, never to watch,

never going back from whence
I came. A few times I wanted

to tell them why I packed
 my belongings and left.

Instead I babbled about salt
percentages in their veins,

in their sweat, in their tears,
wail "we want ice cream,"

please, pick up this faded day.
They're too young for a lesson:

Things end, things vanish, you're
frustrated with the sluggish pace.

Get on my shoulders, piggy-back,
I'll fold your sister under my arm,

a clean towel dampened with shadows,
shielded so they can't see my skull

when it shatters in certainty,
the sea rising up to empty sockets.

Cross Country Family Vacation

Colorado was spinning
I was seven years old
Family drove across country
By Minnesota we were toast
Dad started fining us nickels
for being belligerent

Never gave up Indian heads
before Four Corners
merging to a point
My mother took a picture
Us being miserable—sister crying
My dad feigning a laugh.

When I Think of my Childhood

I think of family, a picture
we hold together perhaps
a painting, the one of fruit

in a bowl. Sometimes when I stare,
I swear I see the soft parts turn
bad, the bruises. On the playground

every apparatus brought fearful results
The jungle gym, my throat choked at a bar
a see-saw comrades leapt off I sat at the top
of a slide, punched all the way to the bottom

At age sixteen, a hundred forty pounds
an empty pit, my ribs stuck out like a step ladder
my toothpick arms with bulbous hinges
I think it impossible to fill my stomach
not that we were wanting, just a never ending

well...To think—was I saved by my
great escapes? I had to come back from
those years later when the Merry-go-round spun
me dry, I woke up late that morning,
still no longer a boy subsisting

living in my head was easy to do, with nothing
to do—the smoke you see raging from my ears
is just my image in the mirror, made quite a sight
of myself. I hoped to be different

Hot Biscuits, Country Ham
at The Loveless Motel

Lumpy gravy is what you can get, scratch
mattress, adorned with three thin blue stripes.

I could send a postcard,
wishing you here—

though you've driven on, past this room
with black mold on the shower stall

a Radio Shack clock radio.
Remember from your teens?

You: rolling onto that first love, how fresh,
almost floral scented, you hungered for

now, biscuits and country ham. A sign flashes
red through worn cloth drapes-tells you so.

There's A Fly in My Soup

Waitress pulls a winged
Insect out from

Wonton Soup
Shifts it between

Pinching fingers
Working as a grinder

Producing blackened ash
Says, "Not fly...seasoning."

THE THURSDAY APPOINTMENTS OF BILL SLOAN

"If Dr. Phil has a show, then why not me?"
~ 2013, Novel excerpt

Inside the Mind of Brad's Therapist

My life's dream is to have my own television variety show, but right now I'm a therapist dealing with the shattered dreams within the lives of others who pay me to solve all their disappointments. I, too, am disappointed. It's ironic that in my dreams I was to go far in life, but instead I'm still living in Massachusetts, the place I was born. The only time I left for any decent period was to receive my Masters of Arts degree at The American School of Professional Psychology in Sarasota, Florida. I had the diploma framed in my office but when things went bad between my wife and me, she came in, pulled it off the wall, and smashed the glass into a million pieces. It seemed each sharp edge that fell onto the carpet was mocking me for the time I've wasted in my life. I haven't spoken to her much since, which I know pisses her off, but I can be a real stubborn bastard if I put my mind to it. Plus now it's sort of become a habit, not speaking to her.

Sometimes I wonder if I should work on my inflexibility. Maybe, I too, need a therapist. Maybe my life would be easier or better. But what's the use? At this point in my life, I can't see what good it would do. It seems every day is the same, and the best way to get through the routine is not to give much of a shit.

I'm talking about my clients, of course. People don't change that quickly, and sometimes they don't change at all, which frustrates me. I have one client, who is only nine, who I might be able to help, but as for the rest of them, basically I just sit and listen, and get paid.

I didn't always feel this way. After I got my PhD, I planned on helping others. I was going to be the caring, sympathetic, insightful therapist who succeeded where all others had failed. I don't have a specialty because I agree that variety is the spice of life, and also it minimizes boredom. I work with bi-polar disorder, multiple personality disorder, substance abuse, anger management, personal evolution, codependency; with men, women, children, groups, and families. I don't want to focus on any specific personality type, disorder, therapeutic technique or treatment, because what I really want, besides being a television star, is to just be free from it all.

As far as seeing both men and women, experts suggest male therapists should see only male patients, and female therapists should only see women. My ex-wife strongly suggests I not see women *period*, but I try not to follow suggestions. I enjoy and respect strong women. At one point, I thought my ex was one of those, but strong women, and for that matter strong men too, are not found in my office. I've got the flawed humans who act out in some way, aggressively or sexually. I'm there to help them realize when this is happening, but it's not my job to prevent any of it. I feel the same way about substance disorders. I know addicts are going to do whatever they are going to do. Who am I to say what is right or wrong, since I engage in some of these activities myself. There is help and a solution for them if they want it, but I'm not going to shadow them to break up drug deals or slap a drink out of their hand. Besides, drinking and drugging may be the only thing that is familiar in their lives. Days pass much quicker if you do things the same way, at the same time each hour, each day, each week and so on. Without predictability we'd all be crazy; which is why I love having a routine so much.

Some of my clients have major anger issues. One is court ordered to see me. I don't know how the courts got my name, but I don't feel I'm the best choice in matters such as this. The courts are pretty stupid, because they ordered him to get treated for his anger problem, but he's not required to show any progress to them. In all likelihood, he won't show any, as he's not coming here on his own free will, nor is he desperate for change. I don't like him very much.

I too, have anger issues.

Who am I? Why can't I have what I want? If Dr. Phil has a show, then why not me? Why not *The Bill Sloan Show*? Last night, I dreamed I was a solid block of concrete with rings of energy flying around me, and the light from the energy was causing all this concrete to crack. I'm not a believer in the meaning of dreams, but when I awoke, I found myself thinking that there is much more in *that* world than in this "real" one, and that if I could crack my blocks wide open, things would be better. Right after that realization, I went back to sleep until the alarm woke me at 7:22 AM. When I got up, I no longer felt the impact of what I had dreamed, which left me feeling angry. The reality of today is that I am tying my tie, tighter and tighter—so tight that it constricts my airway.

GRAND SLAMS: A COMING OF EGGS STORY

"Kenny tapes the drawing of the aliens riding a banana to his mother's refrigerator."

~ 2016, Novel excerpt

Kayak Kenny

When he was a boy, in times of distress and anger Kenny Slatts had been taught by his elementary school counselor to draw something productive and appropriate, as a form of behavioral intervention. Sunday morning, Kenny sits inside his parents' trailer drawing a picture of Joe Keating, complete with a cigarette, a smirking mouth, and a line of cocaine. Beside him is a horribly drawn waitress, who Kenny intended to portray as pretty. Then, holding the drawing up by the corner of the paper, he takes the BIC fine-point, blue, ink pen and slashes it through the paper, right through Keating's heart, leaving the torn artwork spinning away from his fingertips. Kenny, thinking of Keating's training and what Dyed-haired Bob told him, doesn't believe that there will be any change happening within Joe Keating.

Kenny takes a fresh sheet of paper and starts working his pen again, in a more appropriate manner. The yellow BIC fine-tip's point is so sharp it feels like it is not only scratching through the surface of the paper but through his mother's dining room table as well. His drawing arm swoops in an arc, and Kenny starts a picture of a kayak, which more resembles a banana. He sticks some rowers inside, which look more like giant round heads with big bulging eyes that rest on rectangular bodies with little baby arms. The ludicrous Kenny figure is holding a paddle, which looks more like a dialog balloon coming out of his arm. The Kenny figure's eyes are dark and dead looking. Kenny reaches for a red crayon but then remembers the fate of his previous red kayak, almost two weeks ago, and grabs the yellow crayon instead. Upon completion of his masterpiece, Kenny tapes the drawing of the aliens riding a banana to his mother's refrigerator.

When it is time to leave for his 3 o'clock shift, he knocks on his mother's bedroom door. It's 2:15 and his mother is still in bed. It's a good thirty-five minute drive from the trailer park in Peabody to his job at Grand Slams.

Kenny's mom comes out of the bedroom in an old, thin, rugby shirt and a pair of sweatpants she has been sleeping in. Mrs. Slatts walks past the refrigerator, and says, "Oh, that's nice," to Kenny, about the picture, then notices the shredded drawing Kenny made of Joe Keating and holds it up for Kenny to see. "Is this something we do?" she asks. Instead of showing remorse, Kenny screams at her.

"I hate him! I hate him!" Kenny yells. "He tried to get me fired just because he doesn't like me. I think he was jealous that I got the kayak and I asked one of the waitresses to go with me. He said I called the police on him. He's a jerk face!"

"Now, Kenny, none of that type of talk."

"He's an asshole. An asshole! I hate his fucking guts."

"There," his mother said. "Never use the phrase jerk face."

EVERYDAY THERE IS SOMETHING ABOUT ELEPHANTS

"The fish swim to the edge of the glass
to see if I want to talk..."
~ 2018 Flash Fiction

Jack

Jack has no children. There is one person in one frame on the desk. She is frozen there. At the station, everyone is afraid. No one knows what to say. People look for only a second. Jack drinks coffee at work, whiskey at home. He spends the day driving the car fast. Jack arrests some bad people. They live for bad things. It only takes one today to remember the worst thing.

Jack was on duty when it happened. It was all very quick. She had no time to scream. Today he wants a chance at another arrest. He hopes that the guy will act up so he can bash him. The Lieutenant says, take a vacation. Jack says maybe. There is no place to go. Jack wishes he has a chance to use his gun.

Jack takes extra details. Cars stop, cars go all very quick. He is the maestro of an out-of-time orchestra, while his wife was killed. It was all very quick.

Jack has nightmares of yellow tape he can't cross. Jack spends a lot of time on the sofa. It works like a handcuff. Friends bring dinner. There is food on the table. Jack takes off his hat. "Never marry a cop," Jack used to kid. Jack washes his creased face. He says, "Oh, God, Oh, my God."

How Penguins Break

After the first time she slept over his house, Thiesel bought two plastic wind-up penguins, with large blue eyes, the female with long, painted eyelashes. Their fins jutted out at 135 degrees so when you placed them next to each other, they could touch. It was comforting. When she and he wound them, they would clomp around silly and happy, lunging and bouncing toward each other on top of his bureau.

Before they knew one another, they both drank. It was a strong common bond shared in stories they told others about smoky bar rooms, dull eyes, and loneliness. Now, in this moment, there was none of that. They made love five times a day. Slowly pushing into one another felt best, then, as if rewound, they were ready to go again, almost immediately. It was the most amazing lovemaking of their lives. They made up names for new positions and afterward, when Thiesel got up for the bathroom, he moved the penguins; huddled them together. He swore he saw the female batting her bright eyes as her tiny heart beat out of her plastic chest when they hugged each other. Thiesel pulled a tiny red hat she had knitted out of her toiletry bag and placed it on top of Miss Penguin's head.

Then she moved. She had to work in another town in order to survive. The distance was far, and they couldn't see each other as much. He positioned the penguins away from each other on the bureau, their wide blue eyes still locked into each other. Their wanting was horrific. She drank. He told her to hang in there. The next morning he would wake up to find the penguins faced down so he twisted their winders and let them flop around like that sad fish for a while. Often he had to catch them in mid-air when they tried to fall off. Her red hat fell off.

Without telling her he drove to see her, and she wasn't doing well. "It would just be easier if you walked away," she told him.

"I can't do that. I could never do that," he said. "Just come with me and I'll take care of you. You never have to worry again. I'll do whatever it takes to make you happy." He took the penguins out of his pocket, but one of them was broken and could not be revived, while the other bounced around in its silly way but didn't seem happy. He wished things never had to break.

"We could buy new penguins," he said.

"I wish we could just go backwards instead," she said.

He took the one that still had life in it and twisted the winder in reverse until it snapped. He reached for the bottle of whiskey by her bed and she sat smashed on the floor.

What Are The Reasons They Hang On?

The broken-up man said, "That's awful" to the waffle as he sawed his way through it, knife grinding his plate. Then he took the mash and spread it around in a circle before he got up, giving it a thump-thump-thump against the side of the kitchen trash can. The itinerary for the day: coffee, shower, and not a damn thing else.

The phone rings because when things need to be moved along, the phone always rings. "Can you come over," she says, "because he is not dead yet."

"Will he know me?"

"He doesn't know anyone. He's been in hospice, remember? He thinks he's had a good life."

"He must be bad off then."

"Yes."

Shower, coffee, and drive to the Multiplex Nursing and Rehabilitation Hospital. When he sees her, she is in the lobby, not even in the room of the dying father, reading *US* magazine. "Chance of Recovery: Slim and None!" barks the headline, referring to Lindsay Lohan. She looks up over the page spread and says, "You know, it's been nice sleeping with you again."

"Yes, it has."

"I'm afraid I don't know if it's make-up, break-up, or I'm afraid of losing you sex."

"I'm just afraid of everything."

The broken-up man and the broken-up woman bypass the elevator. It is ten flights to her father's room, and he has a briefcase full of books of short fiction. "He can't follow through on a novel or anything longer," she tells him when the shit begins to happen. He holds her hand and tells her that a goldfish was trained to swim through a maze and retained the knowledge months after, yet when the time comes he picks Raymond Carver, Henry James, Andre Dubus, and Richard Yates to read aloud in the beginning of the father's decline.

"You know the end before the end," he says as they follow the colored line on the hospital's polished floor—her shoe slips a bit. Around a bend, she throws the rolled-up magazine into a trash receptacle, grabs his arm for balance.

How Do You Love a Capitalist?

I go on a Valentine's bender buying the super-duper extra-large box of chocolates which barely wedged into a shopping cart, a stuffed teddy bear, cards with gooey Hallmark sentiment, some with funny "bend you over the sofa" quotations and finally ones featuring Mickey and Minnie Mouse.

Then I'm buying pajama-grams and something from Victoria's Secret which can be purchased online and a poem written by Neruda that I'm printing out in red—bold on white paper thicker than what's usually in the printer.

It was during the last snowstorm that I cheated on her; told her I was going to work called the office and said the weather was too rough. When the going gets tough...three dozen roses can be purchased tomorrow, 24 red and 12 white, wrapped up with a necklace with a heart-shaped pendant of tiny diamonds on its border, then breakfast in bed and shit, did I forget anything? How about something for her cat?

I Look At You Through Glass and Water

I imagine my fish have the faces of some of the women I've loved. They are the faces of those I've caused pain to, faces that mock me from a jail-like tank while I stand there staring back at them.

I see Skipper has a tumor right above his tail. His swim is partial and labored. Toots is going blind. I really want him to know everything, to see what is going on outside in the world where everything is as damaged as he is.

What I have learned is that when you are born, you come from the water, but later, when it is over, you're lowered down in the dirt.

And I have learned that when a fish gets sick, you don't flush him because fish suffer in sewer systems for hours, days, or weeks. So when Toots bad eye faces me, I put Skipper the one with cancer in a plastic bag. I place him outside on the ground and pulverize him with my boot again and again...

Inside, there is no giant shoe to stomp down on me when I grieve, so I collapse onto the bed. The fish swim to the edge of the glass to see if I want to talk, but right now, I don't.

Full Moon

Once we saw the moon, big in the sky rising up over the scraggly arms of the shadow of branches. Once we saw the moon lying in the back of my parents' station wagon behind the screen of the drive-in. The movie was on, but we weren't watching.

The moon. It followed us on paths, around ponds we swam in naked after midnight. We yelled to it, asking it to provide heat, the air being cool on a summer night. It just shone brightly back, doing what it did, and I was so proud of the moon in that moment. It made your eyes two points of light, so striking that I stared into them for long periods, and it no longer mattered that we sat in the dirt, sharing a single towel, our bodies warming against one another. I was hypnotized, as you told me all our important things, until you reached for your boots and the trance was over.

Once we saw it from our new home. I said, I'd like to lie on top of it like Snoopy on his doghouse. The doghouse, like the moon tonight, seemed perfectly two-dimensional. It never appeared to actually have a roof, my eyes played tricks every time. My eyes see what I want to see, like when our first child was born, she had light in her eyes, just like yours did by the pond, blessed by God from the Universe. There are so many tricks.

Like the night I saw the moon rise without the two of them. Light was in the window when I walked past to answer the door. I wished the police would stay with me and repeat everything they said after "there's been an accident." I could have saved that. The moon hung in the sky over their shoulders as they spoke, and I looked up to it because I couldn't talk, not even to tell him not to leave because everything else was gone.

I started seeing the moon from the lawn of my empty house. It taunted me, the way it kept coming, and I stared at it with anger, hoping it would explode. I sat inside with the lights off and could not be bothered with something as predictable as its visit every month. Every four weeks, it came to tell me that it was still there, to keep trying; not to give up; and sometimes awful things can happen which you can't control—and that everything else in life continues as normal, whether you like it or not.

Slowly the moon gave back my life. I bargained that I would be willing to do whatever it took to begin to have joy once more. The stagnant gears began to turn, and I began to move forward, slowly creaking.

Thank you. Now, I see miracles I cannot explain. I notice things, a convertible with people jumping up and down, a rock fly, a talking dog, and a cripple walking on water. The darkness sings me a hymn. I am able to see both of you, so clear and sweet, that I hold you in a hug inside my pale arms. The moon lived up to its part of the bargain, and if I'm able, I'll hold up my end.

If We Don't Think, We Will Sleep

I reread *The Little Prince* last night when I couldn't sleep, the world being too large for me. I tried to relate to the book, but since there was no princess in the story, I just wanted to smack the little guy upside the head. I mean, who falls in love with a flower?

Somewhere, someone once said that "love is a rose", so using basic logic, the Little Prince was falling in love with love. Now that's a bad idea, as is talking out loud to a book after midnight when instead I should be trying to sleep. The only thing more frustrating than lying in bed wide awake would be standing up and trying. I was in love with someone who stood pat, so in that way, I fell in love with love as well. That's no good in any book.

Yes, I thought about the time she told me she didn't want kids, but I told her that she'd be such a good parent. She asked me if I really thought so, but I chickened out and said that I hadn't really thought about it much, but I didn't want children myself.

She said, "You're hiding, boy, and soon you're going to be found out," but I told her that she thought too much about thinking, and I knew by giving her that extra fact to think about that all the energy would build up in her brain and would be enough to power a few large cities.

Or, at least, that energy would help keep me awake. When I spoke to my therapist about it he told me that therapists are the worst over-thinkers in the world. "That's great," I said. "Because I'd like to work on being more reserved."

"Would you like a sleep aid?" he asked, but I said, "No, I can get much too reserved that way."

So now, I still don't sleep. Maybe it was I was thinking too much about the note she wrote, which said: "I thought you were pulling away from me, so I'm pulling away first. I love you forever." It was a glorious note because of the basic construction of the message and also its honesty. I checked for punctuation and grammar errors and that too was perfectly spot on. I also checked the rest of the house. She'd left her closet bare all except for a pair of heels, one spike broken, the other standing strong. She owned a lot of shoes, much better than those.

When I walked through the house, I wondered why I hadn't noticed that she took the sofa but left the loveseat. People in love fit better on a sofa anyway, because at least they can lie down together. Only the dust which formed a large rectangle was left behind, but that can be blown away quite easily if I leave a window wide open.

Again tonight, awake, I will lie down and rewrite *The Little Prince* in my head. I will rename it, *The Little Princess* and when the phone rings at 3 AM, it will be her asking, "Can you sleep?"

I'll just say, *yes*, because I know I can.

Everyday There is so Much About Elephants

I'd been told that elephants can change your life. I also had been told that I could change the life of an elephant by protesting the circus. I needed to paint a sign first, but that might be as effective as a candlelight vigil. People like candles, and they march around with Dixie Cups when someone is either missing or dead. When someone dies, a bunch of candles won't do shit.

I spent college starving mostly because I didn't have any edible food in the refrigerator. The elephants ate it. How did I know an elephant had been in the refrigerator? He left his footprint in the cheesecake. That's why it's not edible. Cheesecake would have been nice.

I studied computers and philosophy. I heard the voice of Ganesh when I wrote programs. I never heard, "You look great today" or "Why don't you take a drive to the Cape?" The voices never said, "Have another donut" or "Your professor loves your work." They only told me to kill my parents or someone important like John Hinkley Jr. The voices never said, "It's a sunny day. You should wear shorts."

Anyone remember elephant beer? I got a girl drunk on it once solely for the purpose of getting her drunk so that things might happen. Things did happen. She threw up. I'm not the type to fuck a girl who had thrown up. The next morning she remembered. "I like you," she said. "You do so many things." She became my wife.

I told my job interviewer that I trained elephants. She scratched her head. I needed the job. "But we don't have any elephants here. It's a computer software company."

"I can do so many things," I said because my wife told me that. Training elephants is something you can't get certified for. How would the interviewer ever know unless there were photos from every circus that ever existed. The job paid well, but when the company had a Team Building Exercise at Ringling Brothers and Barnum & Bailey Circus my boss introduced me to Billy Barnum, a friend of hers and a poet. "Well?" my boss said. I recited the only poem I knew, about a gay horse pulling a carriage in the snow. I was fired that Monday. It was interesting timing because usually people are fired on Fridays. That's why suicide hotlines are their busiest before the weekends. If you're fired during the week there is a better chance you'll come back to the office with a gun.

On Monday night I watched *Fatal Attractions*, the show on Animal Planet where people raised exotic animals that grew up and killed them. That night it was about someone that held a baby elephant named Sophie in their studio apartment in Somerville, Massachusetts. It had been born in Africa with only one front leg, which was perfect when it got big and the owner made it stand on its two back legs on his step stool in the kitchen. All the neighbors loved that act until one day the woman in 2-B with a peanut allergy had the Board of Health cleanse the premises for peanut dust. Sophie mashed those guys using her head as a mallet, and then turned on the owner. She hammered him all the way into the building foundation. Perhaps you read that in the paper. If not, it's now on TV.

I left my wife a note after she went to sleep. I drank coffee and drove to New Hampshire, where the gun shops open early, and bought an elephant gun. I had all the paperwork.

"Thar's no elephants up he-ah," he told me.

"That's a joke, right?"

"Yep," he said, and then printed out the receipt.

"I'm buying this gun so that people won't forget me," I said. In life, people aren't good enough. They'll light candles. The elephants won't forget anything.

SPREADING LIKE WILDFLOWERS

"Outside, I invent haikus,
fake free verses or laughter..."
~ 2019 Poems

Bromley's Funeral Home

The old suit jacket's pocket,
housed a tatty funeral card
I pulled out some life
after death, shuddered,

seeing your face creased
on a piece of wrinkled cardstock--you were
so young, but the memory so ancient.
Bromley inserted a few lines

from an ancient Catholic Prayer
printed over a clichéd picture:
Heaven's light beaming down.
Or is it shining up? I can't question this,

or understand a damned thing
about the day of your funeral.
The picture now worth less than
a thousand words unsaid.

The Miracles of Recovery

The body experiences
the mind bending, I was lost

in a body

my mind bent

in such new shapes,
such tension before it snaps.

Who would have thought salvation is no longer
found in the piss jars in old isolated bedrooms?

the mind snaps

the body

quakes its resistance.
I am one step away from

being pushed
in a wheelchair

when my body fails

the mind

perhaps just wilts
as a petal, the rose might—

we are all the stem, we salvage
ourselves from this withering.

Still There Are Boxes

If only we let go, still
 images remain.
Pictures, photos fell
off the wall. The boxes?

Leave them there,
the many only enjoy being
trapped in a room full of people.
It's the way a cage works.

What provides the shade?
There's still a single hair standing
between my eyebrows like
a tree parching in the desert.

Faith

I'm old enough to have dead friends,
And friends with dead friends,
And friends' dead Parents,
dead Children, dead Spouses.

Month old Babies
die, I don't believe,
we will ever see their ghosts.
And if we did, would they stop our hearts?

And would this heart still thrust blood
against opposite walls?

I wonder why
everything has to be.
And I'll never wonder,
if we will go on forever.

And I believe,
one day, I will close my eyes,
to pray—for nothing horrific to happen,
again and again until the very last breath.

At a Cookout for Poets

Outside, I invent haikus,
fake free verses or laughter
about what's on the grill,
and significant other things.

Inside, I imagine my mother's kidney,
is like the old clove of garlic
in the host's refrigerator—
the tumor growing like its root,

pretending, to play polite here,
not to be intrusive, I will ask
God to take care of all
that is rotten.

How to Unring a Bell

An impossible idiom
I tried to solve using
destructive interference.
Can two waves collide

adding up to zero?
We'll try finding silence
by blasting a competing signal.

You thought us as being flawed
like noise canceling headphones,
merely muffling nearby clatter.
So, my darling, you want proof of a how too?

Place a bell in an anechoic chamber,
I'll be the speaker in the middle,
sending an acoustic opposite.

Crawl into the room with me,
Please listen. We are as one,
picking up nothing. Wait, now,
for the caress when the bell is un-rung.

2020 POEMS

"Loneliness was the handcuff.
I wanted bright fireflies instead."
~ 2021 Poems

21 Lines / 2020 / COVID 19

First 1 — person spread to another person in Hubei,
today 2 — house cats tested positive,
and 3 — bodies were found dead in same hotel.
The 4 — main groupings: alpha, beta, gamma, and delta
with 5 —key steps to stop the spread amongst footballers
6 — feet of distance (unless it's ten feet, if people are
running)
7 — trillion dollars in global bailouts
with 8 — corona related scams, beware
of 9 — from a church in Harlem gone, the news reported,
Stephon Marbury found 10 million — masks in China
11 — Alive.com would like to send you push notifications
Regarding the 12 hundred dollar checks — in the mail?
But 13 — deaths a day at a New York Hospital
a pregnant mother's baby, 14 — weeks early, flew out,
as the airline industry, had 15 — deaths the past nine weeks.
A 16 — year-old who was healthy, died in France
17 — corpses were found in a shed, re-named a morgue
after being sick 18 days, the average length of COVID-
19 — for really ill people, will never return
20 — million dollars Ruth's Chris Steakhouse collected on
the 21st — of April, CDC says, the second wave will be worse.

Guesses From a Stable Genius

Supposing we hit the body
with very powerful light,

ultraviolet that hasn't
been checked.

Supposing you brought the light
through the skin or in some way,

you're going to test it
inside the body.

Supposing there's a disinfectant,
that knocks it out in one minute,

something by injection,
almost a cleaning.

Supposing you see it get there,
doing a number on the lungs.

It'd be interesting to check
the way it goes after one minute.

Supposing, that's pretty powerful,
the whole concept of the light.

Kleptoparasitic

Going to heaven, tears
held back, snared,
in hell,

like a fly in a strip, stuck,
a glue tape restrictive,
morphine-like soaring

into the ProZap or skipping Prozac.
The limbo of an insect's life is
a human antonym, perhaps a hymn

of yang and yin, stuck within
majesty of dewdrops,
web affixed, holding

a place. On Earth,
unlike the Theridiidae, we beg
to hold the dying.

Unformed Relief

I took three pills
but they were antibiotics.

I saw my mother stare out vacantly
from a hospital bed, looking for St. Peter.

I overeat.
I under eat.
I never eat

Anymore. Suggestions?
Treat yourself to self-care.

Do something
nice—call your father

who won't remember
losing his car keys

he doesn't remember /
looking for them for two days.

We took them (!) hid them.
Did we save a life?

Ride the haze of mercury,
know where to go.

We know where to go
Do you know where to go?
Tell me where to go.

reply to someone who said
you should write a poem about her
For N.D.

I don't know if I can write this poem
The one about you, the one about...

I don't know—am I deserving of writing something
that's not right? I know, others can, if others can.

I can—pray, *please,* God, someone, write it
someone, God, worthy, or good enough,

but, not me, no, I can't. It's impossible.
You are gone, and it's impossible.

When You Have This Connection

It's like the kitchen is on fire,
when before you only smelled smoke.

you will buy, what you buy, food,
when you buy, if it's what she wants.

You will scrub the house clean
if she were to drop in. No need to call

when you didn't see her on *Wednesday*
as you've seen her the last three of those

like a pattern—a routine you had.
—like laundry on the same night, forever,

always on Wednesday,
the middle of the week.

But the day you sat her down, and confided
you had anxiety about all these changes, you said instead,

"the days are getting shorter, it's getting darker,"
You never liked losing those minutes of daylight.

"Spring always arrives" she answered
yet, I still mourn, like Whitman.

Long Distance Thinking

Loneliness was the handcuff.
I wanted bright fireflies instead—

on-off-on-off-I-couldn't-get-off
the sofa, stuck like glue.

Bought an accordion to make loud bellowings,
gave up and left the large slinky, a toy in the corner.

My dog strays there while I'm not looking,
his tail never wagged quite right, failing

like a helicopter with a crooked rotor mast,
pull me up please, so, *I paused,* his paws pause,

I'd lost my mind half-way through this ride
halfway through my existence, focusing,

trying to picture,
other halves living.

Ballet of Surrender

Dancing, to get up
high, on my toes,
now pointe to each other,
hypothetical anonymity.

High, on my toes,
no one is looking
hypothetical anonymity
I kiss the ground I once fell on.

No one is looking,
now pointe, to each other,
no longer presumed difficult.
Dancing, I am up,

I kiss the ground I once fell on,
no longer presumed punished,
pirouetting won't turn to bellicose
feelings of uselessness, self-pity.

I no longer presumed punished.
I never felt I could be a ballerina,
feelings of uselessness, self-pity,
turn to rejoicing in these basements.

IT SUCKS GETTING OLD

~ 2022, Essay

It Sucks Getting Old

Let me introduce you briefly to Charley Gager

My dad was an engineering egg-head, who worked on the Star Wars Defense system. He counted cards to win Hearts, Rummy, Bridge...had a high winning percentage at Scrabble and a high IQ. My dad had a dry sense of humor, not with the best delivery, but the jokes and puns were delivered in a humorous way.

My dad moved from his home in Massachusetts, to an Assisted Living in Maryland, to when his Dementia worsened, a Memory Care Facility. Two weeks ago when he broke his hip, and his body and mental status became even worse, he went to a Rehabilitation Nursing Home. I just drove back to Boston to where he was in Maryland, and things aren't looking very good—he can't feed himself or get out of bed. He needs help being adjusted in the bed or in a chair which they move him to. He is in pain. He yells out when being touched, and does not know who, what, where, or why any of that is being done. He is only able to be fed pureed food, which in that form, I was unable to identify by color or smell, or anything, what was being served.

Why?

We systematically don't care about our elderly. The people who work as caretakers make minimum wage as the facility takes in the rest. Under paying makes staff people not want to stick around. On the weekend at the Rehab/Nursing Home there were thirty or so infirmed people needed care in phases of indignity and there was one nurse, and one aide. Minimal care which included feeding, which my father needs right now are not possible. So after the Nursing Home Care is paid for, for which you receive people hardly checking in you.

So, Pay More

Our family is spread out across the country, so it is best to pay an additional agency to make sure he gets nourishment. Care.com was looked at, but we had to vet the people ourselves. One, we liked, came back with an outstanding warrant, which was much less than outstanding. Next, up was an agency we used when my father was at Assisted Living. They still had him in their files but it was a different county. The contact was going to refer us to the part of the agency which covers that county, and we were told, if they can't do it, the further county would cover this. Then, days went by. Then more days went by. Then the in-county person ghosted us. Then the original contact person apologized and said they couldn't do it.

Total: 5 days, no care.

Now What?

Another agency got involved and from intake to starting with an aide, it took 6 days (Total: 11 days, no care), which is pretty good. We needed 40 hours, and the hourly rate is $32.60. The aide probably makes minimum wage again, and even with 40 hours of staff, there's going to be turnover. Also, we don't know if they are going to do what we expect, like show up first, and feed him—and get help when needed. We wanted shift notes to be kept in the room so family/staff could read what happened. The extra agency of service said this wasn't possible because of HIPPA and possibly stepping on the toes of the Rehab. Hospital/Nursing Home. All we, the family, wanted was the ability to see if my father ate, or drank...how much and what. Again, it was said this wasn't possible.

Insurance—yeah, good luck?

Medicare doesn't kick in to pay for Hospital Level Care until unprotected money is drained at the rate of $4,000 (low end) to $20,000 a month. My father had bought additional Long-Term Care Insurance which kicked in at 90 days at the Memory Care Facility. Well since he is no longer there, it is now uncovered, and to save that placement, we pay out of pocket starting immediately. Since the Rehab has not served him for 90 days, the policy doesn't kick in there either.

No One Wants to Go Out This Way

My father didn't want to leave this world in this state. He completed á DNR, and did the Five Wishes. His diagnosis is currently not terminal but, based on the care he is receiving, I don't think he'll live another two months. No one I've ever spoken to would like to end their lives in this manner. I've been very vocal about wanting loved ones to snuff me out by suffocating me via a pillow if I ever get to be in that state. My intelligent, humorous and kind father I knew has lost nearly all of his dignity. He never wanted this: being treated as a number, an unknown, a human widget in the quandary of the elderly care system. Even preparing for the end, could not prevent this. The system is broken, and so is my father's quality of life. It's angering, heart-breaking, and devastatingly sad.

You hear it all the time

"It sucks getting old" is a phrase you hear all the time, often after someone pulls a muscle reaching for the bowl of potato chips or something. It's something we make about "us." There is something which happens as well and it's about loved ones, and us taking care of aging parents or family members—where it is observed just how much the care sucks. The pain of navigating through the system where it is take it or leave it—people living their whole life to suffer in the end, and there is nothing you can do about it.

Joe the Salamander

"*Everything is temporary,* the man from the
foster care agency said."
~ 2022, Novel excerpt

Adrian's Prologue

Multiply your age times 365, then add the days from your last birthday until today, and those are the exact odds that the next day will be worse than the worst day of your life. Here was mine: I was at the dining room table working on advanced high school algebra when the police came. I was only 12 at the time. Numbers were my friends. My parents were dead, the police said, and then, to gather my stuff.

I never spoke much to the first foster parents. If I focused on my real parents, I imagined the foster ones might feel slighted. They might not keep me. It was awkward, because all I felt was sad. They bought me new glasses. They bought white button down shirts. Shoes. Books. Toothpaste. *Everything is temporary,* the man from the foster care agency said.

The next three sets of parents were permanent placements. *They didn't work out,* said the same man, who said the exact same thing every time he picked me up from a failed pairing. *No bond was formed.*

I shrugged at him. I never spoke to the man about the times I received black eyes and had my glasses broken. I've moved all over Arizona in the last six years. Not exactly a tour. I couldn't wait to get out on my own.

My final foster parents asked me to plant grass in the desert. The father's name was Walter. I never called him dad. The mother's name I never learned. I called her Mrs. Walter, just to feel I had something on them. I dug the dirt for hours. The seeds didn't take all that much. I knew nothing about growth. The grass that started looked like the random hairs on the top of Walter's head. I watered the yard looking for a miracle. In those days, I pushed my glasses up often because of the sweat, or picked them off the ground after they were slapped off my face. I was a good worker but the goal of work is to produce. Walter told me this while I was pressing a tissue against my puffed out lip.

At Boston University, when I tell Millie this, in her high-rise dormitory on Commonwealth Avenue, she starts to cry. She gives me the confidence to talk and be heard, so she has a role in all this. I decide right there that she is the only one I'll ever tell my story to. I was invited to this dormitory tower last night because I hated the cold, but, really, she wanted me to stay. It's too cold in Boston, but Millie's dorm room is as warm as the sun in Tempe.

When Millie returns from composing herself, I say, "It is too late for any more new parents, and since I'm over eighteen, I'm legally on my own." Millie looks baffled, pauses enough for me to fill the silence. "Look," I say, I've worked hard to get here, applying on my own, and I selected the one as far away as possible from where I lived, on a full scholarship. This is the reason we met. I did this all myself. I plan to go back to Arizona as soon after I graduate, and I hope you come with me. It's warm, and it's what I'm used to." This is what I tell her. I'm not sure if I'm saying the right things.

Timothy Gager

This is Timothy Gager's 18th book. He has had over 1000 works of fiction and poetry published, 17 have been nominated for the Pushcart Prize. His work also has been twice nominated for the Massachusetts Book Award, The Best of the Web, The Best Small Fictions Anthology, and has been read on National Public Radio.

Made in United States
North Haven, CT
09 February 2023

32246835R00211